What Your Colleagues Are ~~~~~~~ ...

Fisher, Frey, and Law take components of effective reading instruction—skills, engagement, relevance—and show teachers how to focus their work in a meaningful way. Plenty of rich, classroom examples from all grade levels illustrate that this work is for everyone!

—Lynn Angus Ramos
Curriculum and Instruction Coordinator
DeKalb County School District

Comprehension inspires me to take action! I want to be deliberate in my selection of texts for students, in my conversations with them, in my questioning, and in my listening to them. We all need to better understand what can make or break a student's motivation: whether it's the *skill, will,* or *thrill*! I want to make book lovers out of my students, and not just create answerers of uninspiring questions with me expecting the same verbiage year after year. Thank you for fueling the fire to go out and do better by students, especially in this era where often we speed through things for task completion.

—Hilda Martinez
NBCT, RTI Coordinator, Literacy Consultant
2020 San Diego County Teacher of the Year

Comprehension challenges the view of teachers as facilitators of literacy activities and begins to demonstrate how teachers can be knowledge builders who break the vicious cycle where students most in need of high-quality reading and writing opportunities end up getting the least. It is particularly relevant for teachers who are working with students that are reading to learn. It illuminates (psychological) variables that can promote a love of reading or contribute to reading avoidance and signals actions that teachers can take to foster a culture of deep reading.

This text contributes to the important debate about knowledge-rich curricula and the role that comprehension plays in an era dominated by smart devices and search engines. The authors elucidate the enduring importance of deep reading as an apprenticeship into ways of thinking and knowing that cultivates what Professor Maryanne Wolf calls cognitive patience: the gateway to contemplative thought, critical analysis, analogic reasoning, and empathy.

—Peter Nielsen
Leadership Development, Literacy and Numeracy (Preschool–Year 12)
Department of Education, South Australia

In their new book, *Comprehension: The Skill, Will and Thrill of Reading*, Douglas Fisher, Nancy Frey, and Nicole Law challenge teachers to rethink the meaning of comprehension with its emphasis on "what and how" instead of offering students opportunities to think about the "when and why." The authors explain the thrill of comprehension, showing how reading can shape our identities, how we think about ourselves and others, how we view the world, and ultimately why we take social action. Carefully, this groundbreaking book guides readers into rethinking and re-imagining strategy application, with an emphasis on quantitative measures of readability over the nuances that qualitative measures reveal. Our re-imagining journey continues as the authors discuss the skills young readers practice to develop fluency and automaticity and those such as vocabulary and background knowledge that continue to grow over a lifetime. Using examples from primary grades through high school, they discuss the teaching of comprehension and students' reactions to the practice that emerges from instruction. They explain the importance of will—student agency—and its relationship to developing literate minds through thinking, questioning, discussing, and problem solving. This is a seminal book that you will read again and again no matter what grade you teach.

—Laura Robb

Author of *Read, Talk, Write* and *Guided Practice for Growth in Reading*

comprehension

douglas fisher | nancy frey | nicole law

comprehension

the skill, will, and thrill of reading

CORWIN
Fisher & Frey

FOR INFORMATION:

Corwin

A SAGE Company

2455 Teller Road

Thousand Oaks, California 91320

(800) 233-9936

www.corwin.com

SAGE Publications Ltd.

1 Oliver's Yard

55 City Road

London EC1Y 1SP

United Kingdom

SAGE Publications India Pvt. Ltd.

B 1/I 1 Mohan Cooperative Industrial Area

Mathura Road, New Delhi 110 044

India

SAGE Publications Asia-Pacific Pte. Ltd.

18 Cross Street #10-10/11/12

China Square Central

Singapore 048423

Director and Publisher, Corwin Classroom: Lisa Luedeke

Editorial Development Manager: Julie Nemer

Associate Content Development Editor: Sharon Wu

Project Editor: Amy Schroller

Copy Editor: Cate Huisman

Typesetter: C&M Digitals (P) Ltd.

Proofreader: Ellen Brink

Indexer: Integra

Cover and Interior Design: Gail Buschman

Marketing Manager: Deena Meyer

Printed in the United States of America

ISBN 9781071812839

This book is printed on acid-free paper.

FSC
www.fsc.org
MIX
Paper from
responsible sources
FSC® C005010

20 21 22 23 24 10 9 8 7 6 5 4 3 2 1

Contents

Chapter 3: *Will* in
Reading Comprehension 63

Chapter 4: *Thrill* in Reading Comprehension 101

Chapter 5: Tools for Reading Comprehension Instruction 133

Visit the companion website at
www.resources.corwin.com/comprehension
to view videos and downloadable resources.

List of Videos

Acknowledgments

Corwin gratefully acknowledges the contributions of the following reviewers:

Melissa J. Black
Associate Dean, Progressive Education Institute
Harlem Village Academy
Washington, DC

Patrick L. Harris II
Teacher
Detroit, MI

Peter Nielsen
Leadership Development, Literacy, and Numeracy
Flinders University
Adelaide, South Australia

Lynn Angus Ramos
K–12 English Language Arts Coordinator
DeKalb County School District
Decatur, GA

Introduction

It's time for a new model of reading comprehension instruction. Research during the past several decades has resulted in significant increases in understanding about reading comprehension itself (e.g., Israel, 2017). Helping students make meaning from texts is critical to their success, and reading comprehension is one of the oldest lines of inquiry in education; Thorndike noted that comprehension required "a cooperation of many forces" (1917, p. 232). Following a comprehensive review of research, Snow (2002) clarified those forces and noted that comprehension is dependent on four variables:

1. *Reader variables*: age, ability, affect, knowledge bases, motivation

2. *Text variables*: genres, format, features, considerateness

3. *Educational-context variables*: environment, task, social grouping, purpose

4. *Teacher variables*: knowledge, experience, attitude, pedagogical approach

Models of reading instruction

But models for helping teachers develop students' comprehension have not kept pace with the knowledge about what comprehension is. While there are strategies such as modeling or reciprocal teaching, a unifying framework for reading comprehension instruction remains elusive. Importantly, reading comprehension instruction should be more than a pile of strategies. The field needs a structured approach to comprehension instruction. We propose that students need to experience reading comprehension instruction across three phases: skill, will, and thrill (see Figure i.1). When they do, students come to see the instructional experiences their teachers provide them as purposeful. Importantly, they begin to accept responsibility for their learning and understand that struggle is a natural part of the process.

Reading comprehension instruction should be more than a pile of strategies. The field needs a structured approach to comprehension instruction.

Figure i.1 A framework for reading comprehension instruction.

Level of Focus	Aspects of Reading Instruction
Skill	Phonemic awareness, oral language, phonics, vocabulary, fluency, and comprehension strategies
Will	Engagement and motivation
Thrill	Taking action and producing

The *Skill* of Reading Comprehension

The forces that must be mobilized to understand a text are many. In this first phase of reading comprehension instruction, teachers focus on the component parts of reading: oral language, phonemic awareness, phonics, vocabulary, and fluency. These components are formulated according to the age and needs of students, with some skills instruction fading as students master them. However, neglecting any one of these processes will very likely result in compromised comprehension. Over time, students increasingly automate these processes, freeing working memory for comprehension. If a student is laboring over individual words, whether because she can't decode them or because he doesn't know what they mean, meaning making is harder and sometimes impossible. When students read laboriously, they rarely pay attention to the meaning and often forget what they read at the start of the sentence or paragraph. Comprehension suffers.

We call these *skills* because we want students to evolve from strategic readers to skilled ones. As Afflerbach et al. (2008) note, "Reading skills operate without the reader's deliberate control or conscious awareness. . . . This has important, positive consequences for each reader's limited working memory" (p. 368). Strategies, on the other hand, are "effortful and deliberate" and occur during initial learning, and when the text becomes more difficult for the reader to understand (p. 369).

At the skill level, specific comprehension strategies are introduced, such as monitoring, predicting, summarizing, questioning, and inferring. Noticing when meaning is lost is a useful skill, especially when the reader has fix-up strategies. Similarly, summarizing information in a text, asking questions during reading, and making inferences likely improve a reader's comprehension of a text.

Importantly, comprehension strategies cannot compensate for lack of background knowledge or vocabulary. Imagine trying to predict or visualize while reading the following sentence from a physics textbook: "Plane potential flow supplemented by the inclusion of circulation is of considerable practical importance" (Joos, 1986, p. 207). You can decode all the words and read it fluently. You even know the general meaning of the vocabulary. But without knowledge of the discipline, meaning is elusive, and knowing a host of comprehension strategies doesn't help.

The *Will* of Comprehension Instruction

When reading comprehension is reduced to a set of skills, many students simply don't read, even when they might otherwise. And we are not just referring to reading outside of school, an important effort for increasing reading volume. We are alluding to students who skim a text simply to find answers, or avoid reading tasks altogether. The *will* level of reading comprehension focuses on students' mindsets about reading. These approaches invite them to engage more fully with texts. Efforts aligned with building the will dimension of reading comprehension center on creating the mental attitude, inclination, habit, or disposition that predetermines a students' willingness to engage in reading. In other words, the will of comprehension relates to student engagement and motivation to read and understand. Reading comprehension instruction oriented to *goals*, *choice*, and *relevance* contribute to will.

> The *will* level of reading comprehension focuses on students' mindsets about reading.

Far too often, students abandon reading when the text is complex. A common misconception is that reading should always be easy, and that struggle must be avoided. In fact, productive failure is widely understood as a necessary component of the problem-solving process. And reading is problem solving. There are times when we grapple with ideas, and we persevere to make sense. That is not to say that first graders should be reading *War and Peace*, but rather that struggle should be seen as natural and that sometimes the texts we read are challenging. Overcoming appropriately challenging tasks fuels a sense of pride and accomplishment, important ingredients in motivation.

> Overcoming appropriately challenging tasks fuels a sense of pride and accomplishment, important ingredients in motivation.

Challenge is crucial for goal setting, itself a powerful influence on learning. After all, we don't set goals for things we already do well.

We set goals for things we want to achieve but have not yet attained. But all goals are not created equally. *Mastery goals* are focused on increasing competence, whereas *performance goals* are focused on demonstrating the skill and ability of a student. Performance goals are much less motivating—getting a good grade on an essay is not likely to increase a student's will to read. Writing a clear and coherent essay is primarily a mastery goal, even though it is also likely to result in a good grade. Helping students establish mastery goals can positively impact their will. We have seen students set goals to understand an Emily Brontë novel (e.g., "My goal is to understand the ways the author uses the unreliable narrator device in *Wuthering Heights*") and with science texts (e.g., "My goal is to use the information in the main part of the article with what's listed in the diagrams."). Students don't independently generate goals like these. Rather, they are the product of success criteria developed by the teacher. Mastery goals that illustrate the criteria for success in the lesson illuminate the incremental progress students are making in their learning.

Another dimension of will in reading comprehension is the use of choice. Sending students home to read the whole class novel is counter to developing their will to read and comprehend. There is nothing wrong with studying texts in class, but increasing choice will increase the number of students who actually read. Imagine focusing on a genre, topic, or theme and creating a list of 10 titles that will allow students to master the standards. Simply increasing choice can increase will.

The Thrill of Comprehension

The final phase of our framework focuses on the excitement that students should experience when they comprehend a text. Thrill in this context refers to the ways in which students can use the information or experience of reading and comprehending in service of something else. We discovered this phase when we started asking students, "What does the text inspire you to do?"

We discovered the thrill when we started asking students, "What does the text inspire you to do?"

Over time, we have come to realize that students need to experience the thrill of comprehension if they are to accept the challenge of developing their skills and putting forth the will to understand. Richard Anderson (personal communication, June 18, 2019), a pioneer in reading research, argued that we needed new metaphors for the purpose, or thrill, of reading. Students should be speaking, thinking, and doing things. Anderson argued that the new roles might be of storyteller, explainer, or arguer.

Imagine the power of writing Amazon.com or Goodreads.com reviews rather than book reports. Or the impact of presenting information to others and seeing something change, or debating ideas or engaging in a Socratic seminar. There are all kinds of ways that students can be invited into the thrill of comprehension. But all of the options we have discovered involve students becoming producers and sharing their thinking with others.

Why This Book

Simply comprehending the text is no longer the point of comprehension instruction. Too many students are stuck at the skill level, with their teachers working very hard to develop students' strengths in this area. A more comprehensive framework for comprehension instruction recognizes that skills are not enough. We would be wise to ensure students' engagement and motivation, developing their will to understand. And, ultimately, we show them that reading and reading comprehension are not passive experiences. Rather, students come to understand that the point of all of this work is to do something with the information. To our thinking, students need lessons on all three levels if we are going to radically change their learning from texts. And that's what we hope to accomplish with this book.

Students come to understand that the point of all of this work is to do something with the information.

The Point of Comprehension Is Not Comprehension

In the introduction, we noted that students needed instruction in the skill, will, and thrill of comprehension. But that may leave you thinking that these are discrete and separate activities that are linear in nature. To dispel that myth, let's take a look inside Bridget Gengler's third-grade class. They were focused on the upcoming Veterans Day. As Ms. Gengler explains, "It's more than a day off school. It's a holiday to recognize some very specific people. Unlike holidays that recognize people who have died, this holiday focuses on people who are alive. Are you interested to know who gets a holiday in their honor?"

The students were excited to get started, in part because Ms. Gengler was enthusiastic, and she made the information sound interesting to them.

There were a number of skills that were taught and practiced throughout the unit. Ms. Gengler had modeled annotation, for example, and students annotated the complex texts that they read. The students had been taught how to take notes and to create graphic organizers (see Figure 1.1 for a sample). They had previous lessons on fluency and vocabulary, including word solving. The students knew that when they encountered an unfamiliar word, they could use context clues, word parts or morphology, or resources. They also understood

Figure 1.1 Student graphic organizer.

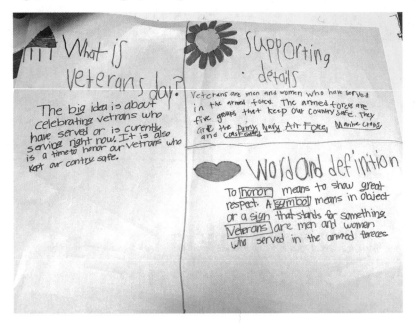

how to summarize information and ask questions. All of these skills were put to the test when they encountered a complex piece of text that explained veterans and Veterans Day.

The skill aspect of the learning was not in isolation. Embedded in the experience was a recognition of the need to attend to the will to read. Ms. Gengler's framing of the lesson helped, but so did the fact that they would have a day off of school the following week, and no one had really explained why there were specific school holidays. They also knew that there was a celebration at their school and that they could present at the celebration if they wanted.

As part of the design of the experience, students understood that they would have opportunities to produce things as a result of their reading. Students were invited to write letters. Some wrote to military veterans; others wrote to explain the day. See Figure 1.2 for a sample letter written by a third grader to a veteran. Some wanted to present at the school celebration; others did not. Some wanted to share their understanding with family members; others wanted to create posters comparing Veterans Day with Remembrance Day, held on the same day in other countries.

Figure 1.2 Sample student letter.

What could have been an ordinary, compliance-oriented task turned into an opportunity to deepen students' understanding about the holiday and, at the same time, allow them to practice their comprehension skills, enable them to build background and vocabulary knowledge, show them that reading was cool, and reinforce their ability to take action in the world. To our thinking, that's what comprehension is all about. As David Pearson (personal communication, 2018) noted, the goal of comprehension isn't comprehension; it's to

> As David Pearson noted, the goal of comprehension isn't comprehension; it's to do something with the knowledge gained.

do something with the knowledge gained. The goal of comprehension is to take action in the world and to make a difference. That's why we all work so hard to ensure that students can, and do, read.

But What Is Reading?

Your eyes are traveling across this page, recognizing shapes and ascribing meaning to those shapes. Are you reading? Perhaps. There is some debate about the definition of *reading*. Is sounding out words reading? Is reading really fast reading?Does reading always mean that you understand and make meaning from the text? Tim Shanahan (2019) forwarded this definition of reading: *Reading is making sense of text by negotiating the linguistic and conceptual affordances and barriers to meaning.*

In this case, reading requires some level of understanding or comprehending. This idea is not new. In 1978 Durkin proposed that comprehension was the "essence of reading" (p. 482). Until at least the 1960s, there was a general belief that comprehension was a matter of intelligence and that smart students who could decode would understand what they read (Duffy, 2002). Therefore, comprehension was not taught. In fact, there was debate about whether or not comprehension could even be taught. Some argue that you don't teach comprehension, you teach *for* comprehension.

Following an extensive review of research, The National Reading Panel (2000) defined comprehension instruction as

> developing students' ability to (a) comprehend the literal meaning printed on the page; (b) interpret authors' intentions to report knowledge, show possession, implied meaning; and (c) evaluate and apply ideas in printed materials to their lives. (p. 76)

Their analysis of 38 studies suggested that comprehension skills can be developed through the intentional actions of teachers. This has led to a resurgence of interest in comprehension, specifically how to teach students to understand and make meaning from texts.

The National Reading Panel's analysis of 38 studies suggested that comprehension skills can be developed through the intentional actions of teachers.

Teaching Students to Comprehend

Knowing *how* readers comprehend should help us design instructional experiences that foster students' *ability* to comprehend.

Unfortunately, there have been a number of false starts when it comes to teaching students to comprehend. Simply understanding the behaviors of proficient readers and then encouraging students to engage in those practices is not likely to produce the desired results. For example, let's look at the "the super six" comprehension strategies: building knowledge and making connections, predicting and inferring, questioning, monitoring, summarizing, and evaluating (Oczkus, 2004). There's nothing wrong with these, and most of us use these as we read. They come from the body of research on the behaviors of proficient and precocious readers—what readers do when they encounter text. Our concern is that these strategies are becoming "curricularized." By this, we mean that the strategies—rather than the text—are becoming the center of instruction. One publisher even markets this curricularization by noting that its program teaches "one strategy at a time." We can't find any evidence for the effectiveness of teaching one strategy at a time, especially with pieces of text that require that readers use a variety of strategies to successfully negotiate meaning.

Models of reading
comprehension
instruction

This was highlighted in a recent classroom visit. We entered a sixth-grade classroom. On every wall there were posters about making predictions: how to predict, what to predict, when to predict, what to record about your predictions, why predict, and so on. Some of these posters were classroom created, while others were publisher-produced. We sat next to Tim, a sixth grader who was reading *Stone Fox* (Gardiner, 1980). We asked Tim what he was doing, and predictably he answered, "predicting." Having read *Stone Fox*, we asked him what he was predicting, expecting a discussion about the dog dying and the family losing the farm. To our surprise, Tim rolled his eyes and said, "Everything, man?" We have to say that it is very unlikely that Tim will incorporate predicting as a habit based on the five weeks his class spent on predicting. We would argue that Tim has developed a significant dislike of predicting and will do just about anything not to predict. Obviously, this runs counter to the goal of the instruction, which is to increase Tim's use of making predictions when they are needed.

We can't find any evidence for the effectiveness of teaching one strategy at a time, especially with pieces of text that require that readers use a variety of strategies to successfully negotiate meaning.

A goal of strategy instruction should be *consolidation*, so that the reader can activate the right strategy (for him or her) at the right time. Consider your own experiences with reading a plot-driven book such as *The Da Vinci Code* (Brown, 2003). We'll venture a guess that you didn't make predictions to the exclusion of everything else. It's likely that you evaluated ("Hmm, not a lot of character development here"), made connections ("I've seen these paintings before"), and so on. In addition, you didn't make predictions at the beginning of the text and then not return to them. Each time a new clue appeared, you revised your predictions. How did you know how and when to do that? Because you were able to consolidate those strategies and activate them when you needed them. A very real danger of curricularized strategy instruction is that the strategies fossilize to the point that readers hold narrow and rigid understandings of how and when they are used.

A second concern related to the increased concentration on strategy instruction is the goal that teachers have for this type of instruction. We believe that the goal should be for students to use these strategies with automaticity, applying them authentically as they read. Afflerbach et al. (2008) argue that, over time and with purposeful instruction, strategies can become skills and that skilled readers should be the goal of instruction. As they note, "Readers are motivated to be skillful because skill affords high levels of performance with little effort whereas strategic readers are motivated to demonstrate control over reading processes with both ability and effort" (p. 372). Another look inside a middle school classroom, this time an eighth-grade classroom, will highlight this concern.

> The goal should be for students to use these strategies with automaticity, applying them authentically as they read. Strategies can become skills, and skilled readers should be the goal of instruction.

Alexandria is sitting at her desk staring at a piece of paper when we enter the room. She has read a passage from the book *Hattie Big Sky* (Larson, 2006), a book she chose to read. Alexandria is required to document on a worksheet the strategy she used to understand the text on a The form is blank, so we ask her "Any surprises so far?"

Alexandria, excitedly, answers, YES! I've been stuck on a word in the book—*honyocker*. The word doesn't matter that much, I guess, 'cause I can read the whole thing without knowing what the word really means. But I wanted to know, so I looked on the internet at home. Here's what I learned: In German, it's from a word meaning hen hunter. In Czech, it kinda means a shaggy fellow. In Hungarian, it comes from a word meaning negligent, careless, sloppy, or forgetful. A long time ago, ranchers in Montana didn't like the homesteaders and they called them honyockers, a mean cowboy slang word. In North Dakota, it means a backward, old-fashioned type of rural person. I feel better now," she says with a grin.

Impressed, we ask Alexandria, known to be a collector of words and a bit of a trivia hound, what the problem was with her completing her work. She showed us the worksheet, which required that she

Focusing heavily on reading strategies can have unintended consequences.

identify one of the "big six" comprehension strategies and she said, "I'm not sure what I did. I read the whole thing, really. I understand it all, but I wanted to learn more about the word *honyocker*. I'm not sure which box to check and what to write. Can you help?"

Again, we were struck with the unintended consequences of the concentration on strategies. Forcing students to independently identify which strategy they use and explain it is not likely to ensure that students develop as skilled readers. Was it monitoring? Sure, she knew herself well as a reader and knew she wanted to mine a specific word. Was it evaluating? Yes, she looked at several websites before settling on one that gave her definitions she found useful. Alexandria had moved into the realm of a skilled reader. Forcing her to deconstruct what was becoming an elegantly automatic process for her was counterproductive.

Forcing students to independently identify which strategy they use and explain it is not likely to ensure that students develop as skilled readers.

Skilled Readers or Strategic Readers

Given our experiences with the nearly exclusive focus on strategies, we question the idea that the goal of reading comprehension instruction is to develop strategic readers. As Afflerbach et al. (2008) noted, strategic reading is "effortful and deliberate" (p. 368) and occurs during initial learning and when the text becomes more difficult for the reader to understand. In contrast, "reading skills operate without the reader's deliberate control or conscious awareness" (p. 368). To our thinking, the goal is to develop skilled readers, those who deploy the strategies they have learned with great automaticity. In other words, they have developed habits that they use almost without thinking about them. And, when texts are difficult, they revert back to known strategies to regain meaning.

As an example, we were sitting near Nick, a third-grade student, as he was attempting to read *Hey, Water!* (Portis, 2019). We selected Nick because he shares his thinking verbally as he reads. His ability to think aloud is strong and thus provides us glimpses into his cognitive processes. At one point, he said, "I'm lost. I don't know what is happening now. I hafta reread." He turned back several pages and started again. Later, he read the large word on the page: *tear.* He pronounced it /ter/. Then he read the sentence in smaller font: *Sometimes you slide down my cheek without a sound.* Nick paused, looking perplexed. Then he said, "That's not right. It's /tir/ not /ter/. Why are those words spelled the same? That's really confusing." Then he proceeded with the rest of the book.

Skilled readers periodically recognize that they have lost meaning, and when this happens, they use fix-up strategies, reread, and so on to regain their understanding.

iStock.com/PeoplesImages

Nick reminds us that skilled readers periodically recognize that they have lost meaning, and when this happens, they use fix-up strategies, reread, and so on to regain their understanding. Most of the time, Nick is a skilled reader. But importantly, he knows how to be a strategic reader when necessary. Thus, to our thinking, the goal of comprehension instruction should be to develop skilled readers.

Before we leave this comparison of skilled versus strategic reading, we would like to return to Afflerbach et al. (2008) one more time. They remind us that comprehension is much more complex than the cognitive skills that we have named thus far. As they note, "The progression from effortful and deliberate to automatic use of specific actions while reading occurs at many levels—decoding, fluency, comprehension, and critical reading" (p. 368). This is an important reminder and one that is often forgotten in conversations about comprehension. Each of those literacy processes is important if readers are going to understand what they read. As we will explore more fully in the next chapter, students must reach automaticity with each of those component parts. As readers develop automaticity with one aspect of reading, they free up working memory to focus on something else.

Building on the work of LaBerge and Samuels (1964), Bloom (1986) explained automaticity as the brain developing its ability to "perform a skill unconsciously with speed and accuracy while consciously carrying on other brain functions" (cited in Wolfe, 2001, p. 102). This is why developing automaticity with decoding and word recognition is so essential to comprehension. Automaticity allows the reader to focus attention on the meaning rather than the process for acquiring the meaning.

Skilled reading versus strategic reading

The question remains: Which skills (or strategies) need to be taught? Importantly, some skills have a finite stopping point, and others do not. In the research world, it's the ceiling effect. For example, once you learn the names of all of the letters, there are no more to learn. You have reached the highest point possible. However, it is unlikely that any of us have reached the top end of our vocabulary development. Just the other day, we learned the word *ganked* from our high school students. (It's to steal something and has replaced *jacked* in the popular vernacular.) By the time you read this, that word will probably be dated, and we will have learned countless new words.

Constrained and Unconstrained Skills

Reading researcher Scott Paris (2005) describes these concepts as *constrained* and *unconstrained* skills. Constrained reading skills are those that have boundaries or limits. There are 44 phonemes in English and 26 letters. As well, there are a finite number of letter combinations that represent the sounds. And there is a limit as to the rate of reading one can sustain without sacrificing accuracy and meaning. These first four reading skills—phonemic awareness, alphabetics, phonics, and fluency—are constrained reading skills. They are

Constrained and unconstrained skills

constrained because we can count them, they are easily measured, and more importantly, they are the foundational reading skills readers must acquire.

However, the ability to decode and read text fluently is not the final destination. If that were so, we wouldn't need to do much instruction beyond elementary school. But true reading is much more than accurate word calling. All of us spend a lifetime acquiring what Paris calls the unconstrained reading skills of vocabulary and comprehension. Unlike constrained skills, there is no endpoint. Your vocabulary is better today than it was five years ago, and your reading comprehension will be better five years from now (see Figure 1.3).

Effective reading instruction involves both constrained and unconstrained skills development. No responsible primary teacher would limit attention to constrained skills only while ignoring vocabulary and reading comprehension. But constrained skills do have a shelf life, in that once they are learned, there is no further benefit to continuing to teach them. Therefore, attention to constrained skills instruction does fade after the first years of school, as students acquire them. In turn, vocabulary and reading comprehension take on an even more prominent role than in the primary years. We include this information because we believe that the skill of comprehending, the focus of the next chapter, requires all of the constrained and unconstrained skills.

All of us spend a lifetime acquiring what Paris calls the unconstrained reading skills of vocabulary and comprehension.

Figure 1.3 Constrained and unconstrained skills in reading comprehension.

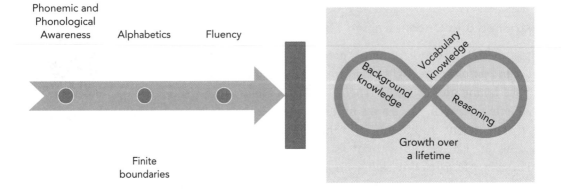

Is Comprehension Enough?

Thus far in this chapter we have reviewed the known. In other words, we have attempted to summarize what the experts tell us about comprehension and comprehension instruction. But we are left with a nagging feeling that, although this is all important, it's not sufficient to ensure that students become readers who choose to read and engage with the world. Several years ago, we started saying that it was time to move reading comprehension instruction from a place of passive reception to active production. Students need to understand what they read, but they need to do something with that understanding. After all, Amazon and Yelp reviews and the countless number of blogs, not to mention YouTube postings, suggest that we all want to share our thinking with broader audiences.

It is time to move reading comprehension instruction from a place of passive reception to active production.

We had been thinking about this when we attended P. David Pearson's retirement party. As part of the event, scholars were invited to share their thinking. At one point, Pearson shared his thinking. We won't get every word right, but in essence he said that teaching students to read includes

Phonemic awareness, which may be important
    if it is on the pathway to . . .

Phonics, which may be important
    if it is on the pathway to . . .

Fluency, which may be important
    if it is on the pathway to . . .

Vocabulary, which may be important
    if it is on the pathway to . . .

Comprehension, which may be important
    if it is on the pathway to . . .

Critical reasoning and problem solving, which may be important
    if they are on the pathway to . . .

Action in the world. Changing something that matters.

WOW. There it is. The point of comprehension is no longer comprehension. It's much more than that. We now realize that comprehension is a step in the process of reading development. It's critical, just like phonics or vocabulary, but it's not the pinnacle. Instead, we need to move to critical reasoning and problem solving, including critical literacy stances. And, we have to ensure that students can do something with their understanding that allows them to take action in the world.

As we thought about this more, engaged teachers with these ideas, and explored the research base, we realized that comprehension instruction needed a new model. Hattie and Donoghue (2016) suggested instructional strategies could be organized along a continuum across skill, will, and thrill, which sparked our thinking about reading. As we noted in the introduction, we believe that there needs to be a model for comprehension instruction. Our model, based on the framework developed by Hattie and Donoghue, is deceptively simple, and includes three dimensions:

- **Skill.** This aspect focuses on the development of the skills necessary for students to comprehend. As we have noted, this includes both constrained and unconstrained skills that are taught to the point of automaticity. This area is probably the most comfortable for most of us, as we have spent decades learning how to teach students the component parts of comprehending texts.

- **Will.** This aspect concerns motivation and engagement. We all know people who can read but don't. They have developed the skills necessary to read yet not the will to do so. There is a lot of evidence for the value of attending to the will of reading as well as evidence about how to develop this aspect.

- **Thrill.** The final aspect focuses on what readers do with the information that they gain from reading. To our thinking, understanding a text should be exciting, especially when there are consequential things that you can do with the knowledge you have gained. Unfortunately, this is rare for most students. They do not find reading to be a thrill, and they see little relevance in reading, as evidenced by the decline in out-of-school reading all of us, students and adults alike, are doing.

Thus, we propose that comprehension instruction needs to be refined and refocused. Students must learn the necessary skills. But their teachers would be wise to focus on engagement and motivation and ensure that students have opportunities to take action and impact the world. We recognize that it sounds lofty, but we believe that nothing less than our readers' futures are at stake. There are far too many lost readers who need to experience new forms of instruction so that they choose to read and choose to take actions that make a difference for them and for their communities. In fact, we will go a step further and suggest that our very democracy is at stake. There is a story, often told, that upon exiting the Constitutional Convention, Benjamin Franklin was approached by a group of citizens asking what sort of government the delegates had created. His answer was: "A republic, if you can keep it." And the best ways to keep it? Separation of powers, such as the three branches of government, and an educated population. Let's do our part to keep this republic we call home.

A new model for comprehension instruction

Skill in Reading Comprehension

"Nothing like a contest to see who might tell the best story," Shane Austin tells his students. "In this next book we'll be reading, there's a free dinner riding on it."

Mr. Austin's high school British Literature students are being introduced to Geoffrey Chaucer's *The Canterbury Tales*, a collection of stories written in the 14th century and told by 24 pilgrims who are traveling together to visit a shrine.

"Here's the thing," the teacher continues. "Chaucer never finished this work, so it's going to be up to all of you to decide who's the best storyteller." The teacher's preparation for this challenging text has been extensive, and he has considered what reading comprehension skills will be vital for his students to understand the text:

- Knowledge about the format and genre of the text, written in Middle English and interpreted into modern English

- Historical information to contextualize the stories as commentaries on the social classes of the time

- Vocabulary, including archaic terminology, references to mythological creatures, and words with double meanings

- A review of satire as a literary form

While the students in his class are mostly reading near grade-level expectations, Mr. Austin recognizes that their reading comprehension skills will be stretched by this challenging text. "I see a primary task I have is in helping my students apply their comprehension skills to more complex literature, not just the stuff they're already comfortable reading." To do so, the teacher's plans for this three-week unit will regularly include ways his students will need to extend their skills in order to understand why Chaucer's 17,000 lines are still considered extraordinary nearly 700 years after they were written.

Not all of us teach Chaucer, of course. But all of us use a ladder of increasing text complexity so that our students can apply reading skills in new and novel ways. Of course, you can't contemplate reading comprehension without also considering the nature of the text. The length, complexity, organization, and topic of the text all influence the extent to which a reader does or does not grasp its meaning. Texts exercise a somewhat fainter but still crucial influence on the will and thrill elements of reading comprehension, which we will explore in subsequent chapters. Our attention for now is on the most recognizable aspect of reading comprehension—the skills needed and their contributions to the proficiency of the reader.

Skill in Reading Comprehension

Skills are highly repeatable and are frequently utilized throughout the reading process (Shanahan, 2019). You will recall from Chapter 1 that for the purposes of instruction, reading skills can be categorized as constrained or unconstrained (Paris, 2005). Together, constrained and unconstrained skills function like pavers on a walkway, each in turn contributing to the traveler's journey. And much like a single paving stone, an isolated skill doesn't get you very far. This should not be misinterpreted as meaning that some skills are less valuable than others. A missing skill makes the path more difficult and can actually impede progress. We'll extend the metaphor just a bit further. Each text is a new journey on a new path. The uniqueness of each text means that the unconstrained skills of vocabulary, background knowledge, and reasoning will be taxed in unique ways.

> The uniqueness of each text means that the unconstrained skills of vocabulary, background knowledge, and reasoning will be taxed in unique ways.

Scarborough (2002), building on the Simple View of Reading or SVR (Gough & Tunmer, 1986), visualized various aspects of reading as strands that combine to create a rope. The SVR suggests that reading (R) is composed of two components: decoding (D) and linguistic comprehension (C). In this model, R = D × C, and if either D or C is missing, then R cannot occur. Scarborough's version focuses on word recognition and language comprehension, each of which has several components. When the strands weave together, the result is skilled readers (see Figure 2.1). As we have noted, these strands are not isolated but rather interconnected, which is why we particularly like this visual. But to foreshadow the upcoming chapters, the will and thrill of comprehension are also important. But without skills, it's hard to have a will or thrill.

Figure 2.1 The strands of skilled reading.

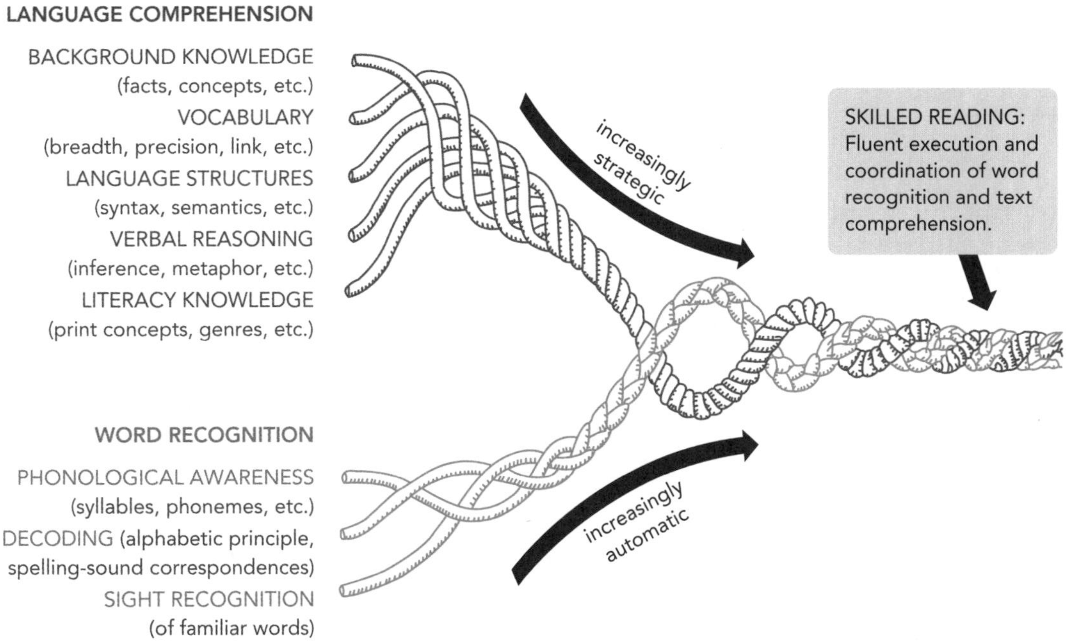

LANGUAGE COMPREHENSION

BACKGROUND KNOWLEDGE
(facts, concepts, etc.)
VOCABULARY
(breadth, precision, link, etc.)
LANGUAGE STRUCTURES
(syntax, semantics, etc.)
VERBAL REASONING
(inference, metaphor, etc.)
LITERACY KNOWLEDGE
(print concepts, genres, etc.)

increasingly strategic

SKILLED READING:
Fluent execution and coordination of word recognition and text comprehension.

WORD RECOGNITION

PHONOLOGICAL AWARENESS
(syllables, phonemes, etc.)
DECODING (alphabetic principle, spelling-sound correspondences)
SIGHT RECOGNITION
(of familiar words)

increasingly automatic

Source: Scarborough, H. S. (2002). Connecting early language and literacy to later reading (dis)abilities: Evidence, theory, and practice. In S. B. Newman & D. K. Dickinson (Eds.), *Handbook of early literacy research*, p. 98. Guilford Press. Reprinted with permission.

Of course, all of the skills we focus on in this chapter are mediated by knowledge. How much readers know impacts their understanding. Before focusing on the specific skills that must be taught, let's explore the ways in which background knowledge influences readers and reading.

Background Knowledge in Reading

Background knowledge in reading.

Consider your reading experiences in the past week. You undoubtedly read texts directed at educational professionals such as yourself. But you may also have read a daily news outlet to keep up on a current event, consulted a few websites to locate a new recipe to try out, checked out a review of a film opening this weekend, and caught up on how a sports team fared in last night's game. Your relative knowledge of world events, cooking, film, and sports mediated your comprehension of each of these texts. Yet it also exposed the background knowledge you don't have. It is unlikely that a diplomat, a chef, a movie producer, or a sports journalist would have found the same readings to be satisfactory. Their extensive knowledge of their respective fields fuels their pursuit of more complex texts that will address their needs. The same texts that would be a better match for them would probably be too technical for casual consumers like the rest of us. In turn, the professional documents you read this past week would likely confound them, too.

David Ausubel, one of the premier educational researchers of the 20th century, said this about background knowledge:

> If I had to reduce all of educational psychology to just one principle, I would say this: The most important single factor influencing learning is what the learner already knows. Ascertain this and teach him [or her] accordingly. (Ausubel, 1968, p. vi)

Background knowledge that lies dormant and unused by readers will not elevate their understanding of the text.

One's knowledge about a subject can mediate one's ability to comprehend written text about the topic. Note that we say *can*. Background knowledge that lies dormant and unused by readers will not elevate their understanding of the text. Readers who utilize their background knowledge more efficiently are able to comprehend more complex texts. Keep in mind that reading is about acquiring and extending knowledge of the physical, social, and biological dimensions of the world. The National Research Council's report entitled *How People Learn: Brain, Mind, Experience, and School* offers a frame for how we use our prior knowledge to learn about the world:

> The new science of learning does not deny that facts are important for thinking and problem solving. . . . However, the research also shows that "useable knowledge" is not the same as a mere list of disconnected facts. Experts' knowledge is connected and **organized** around important concepts . . . it is **conditionalized** to specify the contexts in which it is applicable; it supports understanding and **transfer** to other contexts rather than only the ability to remember. (Bransford et al., 2000, p. 11, emphasis added)

Those three characteristics of background knowledge form the core of knowledge's role in reading comprehension. To summarize,

1. Knowledge must be organized.

2. Knowledge must be conditionalized.

3. Knowledge must be transferred.

Knowledge Must Be Organized

Most of us have watched a student fumble though a messy backpack or desk in a futile attempt to locate an item. She is sure it is in there, but she can't find it. Knowledge works in a somewhat similar fashion. Without some means of organization, information is ephemeral—here one day and gone the next. In the case of knowledge, the organizer is schema. Here's another metaphor for thinking about schema. Dump 100 paper clips on the table, and you have a random mess. A pile of paper clips that isn't organized is much like the knowledge in a student's head—it isn't readily accessible. But hold a magnet over those same paper clips and watch how they instantly attach themselves as a single unit. Schema works like the magnet—it draws together otherwise disparate information to function in a more coherent way.

When building background knowledge, effective teachers know to move from the *known* to the *new* in order to activate existing

When building background knowledge, effective teachers know to move from the *known* to the *new* in order to activate existing schema.

schema. Third-grade teacher Ana Raka's students are studying social and group behaviors of organisms. They will be reading an informational passage on migratory patterns of monarch butterflies. In order to activate and organize their schema, Ms. Raka draws on what they have already learned.

"We've already looked at other living things to see how living in a group helps them survive. Let's make a list of examples we already know," she says. In short order, the class collectively lists ants, dolphins, wolves, and bats as previously studied organisms that live in groups.

"Those are great examples," says Ms. Raka. "Now we're going to read about a different organism, the monarch butterfly. They come together as a group for a short time, and they do so to migrate thousands of miles. As you read about them, I want you to be thinking about ways their behavior is alike and different from these other living things we've already listed." The teacher's plan for the lesson includes coconstructing a graphic organizer to make the comparisons. "They may decide that a Venn diagram will work best for this purpose, but I want to give them experiences with ways to organize their thinking."

Knowledge Must Be Conditionalized

Knowledge is commonly described as having three levels, and instruction typically follows a path from one to the next: declarative knowledge, procedural knowledge, and conditional knowledge (Brown, 1987) (see Figure 2.2).

- **Declarative knowledge** is factual and is the "what" of learning. An example in reading is knowledge of strategies such as summarizing. A reader with declarative knowledge of summarizing knows that a summary is brief and captures the main idea and key details.

- **Procedural knowledge** is the "how" of learning. A reader with procedural knowledge of summarizing can gather and write sentences that accurately summarize a reading.

- **Conditional knowledge** fosters expertise, as it is the "when and why" of knowledge. A reader with conditional knowledge of summarizing makes accurate decisions about when summarizing is useful even without teacher prompting.

Unfortunately, too often reading comprehension skills instruction emphasizes the "what and how" and provides little opportunity for students to get to the "when and why" stage of knowledge. A curricularized approach to reading comprehension strategies instruction, which we discussed in Chapter 1, reinforces a narrow understanding, as students are falsely led to believe that you use only one skill at a time. In other words, six weeks of summarization instruction without attention to how other strategies are utilized doesn't do any favors to students. Of course, students should be taught reading comprehension strategies with intention. But once students have been taught the declarative and procedural knowledge of comprehension strategies, our work must shift to growing their conditional knowledge capacity. This means utilizing these with increasingly complex texts, and continually interleaving instruction so that students are able to think flexibly.

> A curricularized approach to reading comprehension strategies instruction reinforces a narrow understanding, as students are falsely led to believe that you use only one skill at a time.

Interleaved instruction is the practice of mixing topics, or in this case reading comprehension strategies, to strengthen learning and deepen schema. "I make sure I jumble things up even when we're

Figure 2.2 Types of knowledge and their functions.

Type of Knowledge	What Is It?	What It Does	Example
Declarative	Definitional level learning that answers "what"	Entry level factual knowledge that builds initial understanding and early categorization	A reader can define what a mnemonic is.
Procedural	Process level of learning that answers "how"	Application of a procedure such that the learner can accurately and reliably replicate it	A reader can accurately develop a mnemonic when prompted to do so.
Conditional	Problem-solving and decision-making level of learning that answers "when and why"	Strategic and fluent use of procedures for the purpose of resolving problems under a wide range of circumstances	A reader recognizes when a mnemonic would be useful and develops one in order to memorize important information.

just learning a new tool," explains kindergarten teacher Daniela Royce. Her students are learning about question generation in text, but Ms. Royce is making sure to interleave previously learned strategies such as making predictions and setting purposes. During an interactive read-aloud of the book *The Doorbell Rang* (Hutchins, 1986), Ms. Royce prompts her students at various stopping points to formulate questions. However, the story lends itself to lots of prediction opportunities, so she also pauses to solicit predictions from her students. At one point when the discussion stalls, she returns back to an earlier discussion about the purpose of the story. "It is going to take lots more experience for them to get to the point where they can use these cognitive tools on their own. It will take years, in fact. But it begins with them having lots of chances to use comprehension strategies to resolve meaning," said Ms. Royce.

The kindergarten teacher's colleague, fifth-grade teacher Rita Andrade, appreciates the foundation Ms. Royce establishes. "At this point, my students have learned about reading comprehension strategies and how they can be used," Ms. Andrade explains. "My attention is increasingly on utilizing them with challenging texts." Noting how important monitoring one's understanding is, Ms. Andrade emphasizes being conscious of when a difficulty presents itself. "My informal conferences usually include conversation about when they encountered a difficulty and what they did to address it. I want them to be metacognitively aware."

Ms. Andrade stopped to talk with Booker and Owen about an article they were reading in their social studies class on the Iroquois League of the Six Nations.

"Were there any places that got bumpy?" the teacher asked Booker.

"Yeah," replied the boy. "I got confused in this paragraph when they were describing dugout canoes and it said the boats were 'elementary' so then I was like, 'You mean school?' But I knew that wasn't right."

"You were right that your definition didn't make sense," Ms. Andrade said. "How did you fix it?"

Booker explained that he reread the paragraph and found a context clue that explained that the canoes were simple and were not preferred transportation of the Iroquois. "They liked to travel by land, not by water," Booker said. "So, then I thought about what I knew about elementary, and that it is like the beginning of school. It's not the end, but it's how we get started."

"So, you noticed that something didn't make sense. You looked back in the text and found a context clue, then you thought about other possible meanings of a familiar word," Ms. Andrade summarized. "Nice! How about you, Owen? Did you have a problem with that passage, too?"

Owen nodded. "Yes, but I did something else. I looked at the heading and turned it into a question. So then in my mind it said, 'How did the Iroquois travel by land and water?' Then I saw that it was a compare and contrast, so I had to figure out what comparisons the author was making. I also looked ahead and saw the picture with the caption about snowshoes and sleds and read about how important it was for them to have good ways to travel in the winter. So, I inferred that land travel was more important."

The teacher was impressed with both boys. "Owen, you solved a problem in a different way. You looked ahead, changed the heading to a question, thought about the text structure, and did some inferring. And that's the point. There are lots of tools you could use. The two of you used different reading strategies, but you were both successful. Really well done!"

Knowledge Must Be Transferred

The ultimate goal of education is to promote transfer of learning to new and novel situations. Perkins and Salomon (1992) describe transfer across two dimensions: near transfer and far transfer. Near-transfer learning is easily spotted. A child learns the sound and sight of the consonant blend /sw/ and uses that knowledge to read *swim, swat,* and *swish.* Another example of near transfer is when a student learns the meaning of *rudimentary* and applies that knowledge to understand the following sentence: *The design of Robert Goddard's first solid-propellent rocket was rudimentary at best.* Teachers create initial application opportunities that hug close to initial instruction so that learners can practice new skills using examples designed to hew closely to the original. During near-transfer learning, the teacher provides lots of examples using modeling and thinking aloud, and students summarize their growing knowledge.

One method for promoting far transfer involves engaging in interdisciplinary instruction of a text in two different subjects.

But far transfer requires different instructional techniques that bridge a learner's application of knowledge in new and original ways. One method for doing so is to engage in interdisciplinary instruction of a text in two different subjects. Middle school teachers Jeff Bonine (science), Thomas Tutogi (social studies), and Bryan Dale (English) collaborated in an interdisciplinary series of lessons using the core text *Hatchet* (Paulsen, 1986). While Mr. Dale taught using the novel about a boy who survives a plane crash in the remote Alaskan wilderness, Mr. Bonine examined the science behind the protagonist's survival experiences, including mosquitoes, building a fire, and enduring a tornado. Mr. Tutogi led the students in a parallel examination of another real 13-year-old's story of endurance as she and her family hid from Nazis. *Anne Frank: The Diary of a Young Girl* (Frank, 1993) served as a way to contrast the threats of nature faced by Brian with the human threats Anne confronted. Their instruction varied considerably from that associated with near transfer, as they promoted reading across documents, and they encouraged students to develop metaphors and analogies to compare the two adolescents, and to apply their knowledge of science to examine the plausibility of Brian's survival. In addition, the students were also applying their knowledge of reading comprehension strategies in challenging texts.

Background knowledge is one of the mediators of comprehension, to be sure. But students have to read the text as well. Let's start with the constrained skills that underpin reading. These foundational skills are crucial for readers to master. Without careful attention to the development of the sounds and symbols of the language, development of the unconstrained skills of reading comprehension are inhibited and result in learners who fail to make expected gains.

iStock.com/FatCamera

The Sounds of Language

Five-year-old Mateo and his classmates believe they are playing a game, but their kindergarten teacher Lisa Jacobs knows better. Every morning, she leads her students through a fast-paced routine to build their phonological awareness. Her students chant familiar rhymes about the day, clap syllables of longer words, and count words in poems. At the moment, the teacher is leading them in the Take a Trip game. Ms. Jacobs brings out a small suitcase covered in letters of the alphabet and opens it so the students' view is blocked. "Today I'm taking a trip on a train," she begins, "and the conductor told me to put all these sounds in my luggage."

The sounds of language

Mateo and the others know what's coming next—they need to listen closely in order to figure out what the secret sound is for this trip. "I'm going to put a *pot* in here," she says, pretending to place an invisible pot in the suitcase. "And I'm going to need a *mop*, too," she says. "I can't forget my *dog*," she adds, elongating the word just a bit. "Let's see, I've got a pot, a mop, and a dog in my suitcase. Oh, and I need a *sock*," she adds. "A pot, a mop, a dog, and a sock. Tell your neighbor the secret sound."

Mateo and the others whisper to each other, making the sound of short /o/.

"Let's make the sound together, and really loud so they can hear us all through the train!" she says. "What other words have the sound of short /o/ in the middle?" she asks. "I'll list them for us." In the next few minutes, the students name *cop*, *not*, *job*, and *doll*, and she encourages them to identify rhyming words to pair with each.

These kindergarten students are benefiting from explicit daily instruction to build their phonological awareness. The term *phonological awareness* describes elemental factors of the sounds of language and one's ability to manipulate those sounds, or what Fitzpatrick (1997) calls "the ability to listen inside a word" (p. 5). These factors occur at four levels (see Figure 2.3):

- *Sound level (phonemic awareness)*
- *Word level*
- *Syllable level*
- *Rhyme level*

Figure 2.3 Components of phonological awareness.

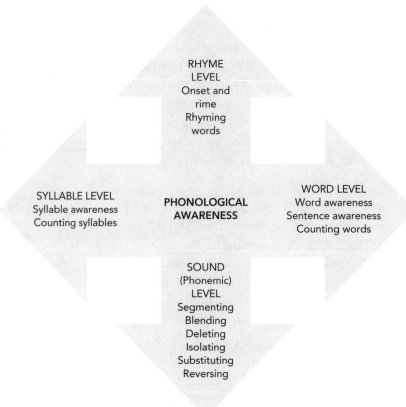

The sounds of a language form its building blocks for the written form. Young children need to perceive and be able to manipulate oral language in order to understand how these same concepts are represented in print. A child who cannot detect and manipulate the sounds of the language will have difficulty in sounding out words for reading or writing. There are five levels of phonological awareness (Adams, 1990). The first four levels are generally mastered by the end of first grade, while the fifth level typically extends into fourth grade. This is a common misconception, as teachers beyond the primary years may not realize that their elementary students are still refining their phonological awareness and thus may be hindered in their reading growth (see Figure 2.4).

A child who cannot detect and manipulate the sounds of the language will have difficulty in sounding out words for reading or writing.

Figure 2.4 Levels of phonological awareness.

Level of Phonological Awareness	Definition	Example
Level 1	Hearing rhymes and alliteration	Perceiving the rhythm and rhyme in "Hickory dickory dock, the mouse ran up the clock"
Level 2	Oddity tasks, such as figuring out which word in a string does not rhyme	Knowing that the word *paste* is the oddity in the sequence *race, vase, place, face,* and *paste*
Level 3	Blending words and splitting syllables	Listening to the sounds of /m/ and /āl/ to say *mail*; recognizing that *mailbox* consists of two syllable sounds
Level 4	Orally segmenting words. This is the opposite of blending words, a Level 3 skill.	The student, upon hearing the word *weight*, can isolate the three phonemes (/wāt/).
Level 5	Manipulation tasks that require the ability to delete, substitute, add, and reverse phonemes	An example of a phoneme reversal is *tell* and *let*.

Phonological awareness skills are primarily taught through a variety of word play games, including chants, songs, poetry, and short daily routines.

Sound-Level Instruction

The first level of phonological awareness is at the individual sound level and is called *phonemic awareness*, which is a subskill of phonological awareness. Phonemes are the smallest units of sound present in a language, and in English there are 44 phonemes. Spanish has 24, while !Xóõ (pronounced /kō/ in English) has 112 phonemes and is spoken primarily in Botswana. As noted in Figure 2.5, the manipulations of the sounds range from segmentation and isolation of individual sounds to reversals. Young children typically learn to attend first to the initial phoneme in a word, such as recognizing

Phonological awareness skills are primarily taught through a variety of word play games, including chants, songs, poetry, and short daily routines.

that *map, moose*, and *Megan* all begin with the same sound. Final sounds follow shortly thereafter, such as when a student accurately identifies that *lamb, Mom*, and *time* end with the same sound. Medial sounds are the most challenging, and Ms. Jacobs's Take a Trip game encourages her students to listen for the middle sound of short /o/ in the words *pot, mop, dog*, and *sock*.

Word-Level Instruction

The sounds of spoken language, including its pauses, are represented in print, too. Voiced words are separated by a millisecond of silence; written words are separated by small spaces. Young readers who detect the pauses in spoken language will more readily recognize that space carries meaning in written language.

Word-level instruction for phonological awareness includes saying to students, "Listen to my sentence and count the words you hear. How many are there?"

Compound words similarly require blending, such as blending the words *ground* and *hog* together to make *groundhog*, then separating them once again into two separate words, and deleting one to isolate the other word. "Let's clap the words. One clap for *ground*, then another clap for *hog*."

Repeat these several times, each time shortening the pause between each. "Now let's put the two words together to make a new one. Clap twice—*groundhog*." After pulling them apart orally, ask students to delete one word.

"What do we have when we say *groundhog* without *ground*? Without *hog*?"

Syllable-Level Instruction

A syllable is an uninterrupted unit of speech, usually with a vowel sound, and may be an entire word (*sun*) or a segment of a word. (*Sun-* and *-ny* are the two syllables in the word *sunny.*) Children use syllable knowledge to work their way through print words and to pronounce new words. Young students love big words, and stories and songs that feature multisyllabic words are an opportunity to draw their attention to this feature of language. Counting the number of syllables in Rumpelstiltskin's name or the names of dinosaurs (e.g., *velociraptor* and *diplodocus*) provides students with opportunities to segment, isolate, and blend sound units.

Rhyme-Level Instruction

Rhymes provide children with a multitude of ways to manipulate sounds. Segmentation exercises for onset and rime structures are especially valuable for developing this skill. An onset is the first consonant sound in a word, while the rime is the remainder of the word (see Figure 2.5 for examples). As they must with the other dimensions of phonological awareness (sound, word, and syllable levels), students must learn to isolate, segment, blend, delete, and substitute sounds to generate rhymes. Songs and poems are a natural place to find lots of rhymes. In addition, word play such as I Spy ("I spy with my little eye something in this room that rhymes with *rock*") and

Figure 2.5 Common onset and rime structures.

Word	Onset	Rime
bun	b-	-un
rate	r-	-ate
short	sh-	-ort
tight	t-	-ight
quest	qu-	-est
yoke	y-	-oke
chalk	ch-	-alk

picture rhyming ("How many words can we think up that rhyme with this picture?") require students to mentally consider the sounds of what they are viewing, further strengthening their phonological memory. This ability to hold sounds consciously in working memory is critical in reading.

These same processes of sound-, word-, syllable-, and rhyme-level knowledge are critical for older students who have not mastered the sound of the language. Ying Yue is a seventh-grade student recently arrived from China. She and her parents moved to the United States to accept a new job with an international firm. However, the girl's knowledge of the sounds of English is minimal, and although she is a strong reader in Mandarin, her heritage language, she needs phonological instruction in order to better leverage her literacy skills in the new language. Some English sounds are not used in Mandarin, such as /v/, /z/, and consonant clusters like /dr/, /pl/, and /st/. Further, words in Mandarin are monosyllabic, with the meaning changing depending on the tonal variation (high level, rising, falling–rising, falling, and neutral; Cheng, 1991). Mark Niu, the bilingual specialist who works with Ying Yue, and her classroom teacher use age-appropriate word games to build her phonological awareness of unfamiliar sounds. Mr. Niu and Ying Yue list food words that contain targeted sounds, then write a short dialogue that includes these words. "It gives her the chance to produce sounds in an authentic way," says Mr. Niu.

She also works in small groups with him. Mr. Niu has students use matching games of photographs and words or sentences. Some students are given photos downloaded from popular websites about movies, video games, and music, while others have sentences that describe the photos. These sentences contain targeted sounds, and students repeat the sentences to build their knowledge of unfamiliar sounds.

The ability to attend to the sounds of the language is crucial for emergent reading development, whether in a first or subsequent language. These sounds are paired with the visual symbols of the language through careful attention to phonics instruction.

Phonics: Sound and Print

Phonics instruction is the process of bolting the sounds of the language to the written symbols of the language. Readers use what they know about the sounds of language (phonemes) to translate the letters and letter combinations (graphemes) to decode written text. As with phonological awareness, this should never be left to chance. Reading isn't a "natural" process. Unlike spoken language, the brain is not hardwired to acquire the ability to read (e.g., Dehaene et al., 2015; Wolfe, 2001). The early stages of reading development mark profound biological changes in children's brains as they learn to coordinate several neural networks. Chyl et al. (2018) studied brain activation patterns of 111 prereaders and emergent readers using *f*MRI data and determined that "a child's brain undergoes several modifications to both visual and oral language systems in the process of learning to read. [The results] also suggest that print-speech convergence is a hallmark of acquiring literacy" (p. 76).

Reading isn't a "natural" process. Unlike spoken language, the brain is not hardwired to acquire the ability to read.

Phonics instruction begins upon entry to school and includes the names of the letters of the alphabet and their associated sounds. Visual discrimination among letters is vital, as the detection of minute changes in letters (e.g., d, p, q, and g) is necessary in determining the difference between *dale*, *pale*, and *gale*. Letter-sound relationships in English are not limited to one-to-one correspondence, as the 26 letters of the alphabet are used to represent 44 phonemes. Thus, students must also master digraphs, each of which makes a unique sound (*gr, ng, sh, th*, to name a few), and diphthongs or gliding vowels (e.g., *oy, oi*, and *ow*). Young readers are further challenged to match sounds to trigraphs (e.g., *sch, nth, thr*, and *squ*) and to r-controlled vowels (e.g., *or* in *cork*, *ir* in *third*, and *ur* in *curl*).

Phonics Instruction

Phonics should be taught with intention, and with a clear scope and sequence so that all children are receiving explicit daily instruction. There is well-deserved criticism of literature-based curricula of the past that did not include a strong phonics component, relying instead on chance occurrences and discovery learning. As Doug likes to say, "We don't need to waste a child's time hoping he discovers that the letter *s* makes the /s/ sound." However, nearly all contemporary comprehensive reading curricula come with a scope and sequence of phonics instruction. The design of these programs should follow the National Reading Panel's recommendation that

There is well-deserved criticism of literature-based curricula of the past that did not include a strong phonics component.

iStock.com/FatCamera

systematic phonics instruction, "a planned, sequential introduction of a set of phonics elements along with teaching and practice of these elements," is necessary for reading acquisition (National Reading Panel, 2000, pp. 2–89).

Having said that, it is the teacher's responsibility to ensure that robust daily phonics instruction occurs.

When using a synthetic phonics approach, students' attention is brought to each letter in a word from left to right. Moreover, letters are taught not only in the initial position of a word but also in the medial and final positions.

Types of Phonics Instruction

Phonics instruction draws on three distinctive approaches to help students acquire the skills needed to decode accurately and fluently. The three are synthetic phonics, analytic phonics, and analogic phonics, and learners benefit from judicious use of all three.

Synthetic phonics, which aligns most closely with the Simple View of Reading (Gough & Tunmer, 1986) uses a part-to-whole approach to learning the relationship between phonemes and corresponding letters and letter combinations. When using a synthetic phonics approach, students' attention is brought to each letter in a word from left to right. Moreover, letters are taught not only in the initial position of a word but also in the medial and final positions. Attention to reading each word across the word provides students with opportunities to blend and segment letters and corresponding sounds, while focusing on each element of the word (see Figure 2.6).

Unlike synthetic phonics, which focuses at the phoneme level, *analytic phonics* attends to larger sound units (phonograms). Thus, a teacher may begin with a phonogram such as *-ook* to build the words *book, cook, hook, look*, and *shook*. If this sounds a lot like the onset-and-rime component of phonological awareness, you're right. This is a top-down approach, and in combination with the bottom-up intention of synthetic phonics, it further strengthens the child's ability to manipulate letter-sound correspondences.

Figure 2.6 Types of phonics instruction.

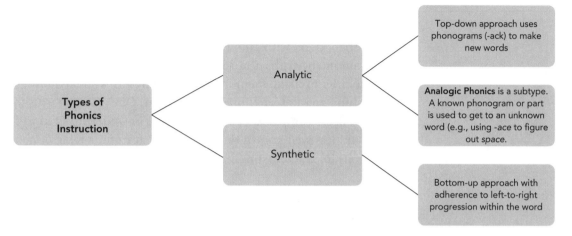

Analogic phonics is a subtype of analytic phonics and is used to assist students in using known words to get at unknown words. For example, a student may know the word *owl* but stumbles on *growl*.

The instruction is focused on two elements—reading the entire word from left to right, and utilizing the part that the student already knows. This should not be confused with guessing at a word— we never want students to simply guess. Rather, the intention with analogic phonics is to help the reader locate and consolidate the information she has in order to take on a new word.

Unlike synthetic phonics, which focuses at the phoneme level, analytic phonics attends to larger sound units (phonograms).

As discussed in Chapter 1, automaticity is essential to reading. Rapid automatized naming (RAN) is a measure of a child's ability to name letters, words, and nonwords (also colors and numbers) quickly and is a predictor of decoding and comprehension (Araújo et al., 2015). Therefore, daily phonics instruction should include opportunities for spaced practice and overlearning. *Spaced practice* provides short periods of intensive rehearsal at regular intervals. Attention each day to phonics development ensures that students are practicing at a pace that aligns with the learning sciences. *Overlearning* is what builds automaticity, as the student continues to rehearse known skills in order to make them increasingly efficient while requiring a diminishing amount of effort and attention. One example is using flashcard decks composed of mastered letters or words mixed in with newer and less well-known ones. Figure 2.7 features a table of considerations for teaching phonics.

Figure 2.7 Considerations for teaching phonics.

Practice	Considerations
Teach students to recognize and write single letter-sound correspondences.	Introduce letters that are very dissimilar in sound and appearance (e.g., /a/ and /t/) and gradually narrow the contrast in sound and appearance (e.g., /b/ and /d/).
Introduce short vowels and long vowels early so that students can form simple words.	Consonant-vowel-consonant (CVC), CVCC, and CVC-e words (silent e) compose most of the words in decodable and vocabulary-controlled texts.
Teach students to recognize and write blends, vowel and consonant digraphs, and more complex letter combinations in words.	Begin by introducing easier combinations such as /sh/ and /th/, progressing through vowel digraphs such as /ea/ and trigraphs such as /ght/ and /thr/.
Use explicit instruction of phonics to ensure all students are progressing at expected levels.	Use modeling with think-alouds and direct instruction to introduce skills. Use repetition, deliberative practice, and application through oral and written language to build automaticity.
Use synthetic, analytic, and analogy-based approaches to phonics instruction.	Young children benefit from each of these approaches, as each shows students how words are decoded.
Integrate phonics skills and knowledge into connected texts.	Deepen phonics knowledge by highlighting its use to decode familiar and unknown words in reading materials.
Teach to automaticity.	Students must develop automaticity in decoding in order to gain the cognitive space needed to comprehend and make meaning.

Source: Fisher, D., Frey, N., & Akhavan, N. (2020). *This is balanced literacy grades K–6,* p. 47. Corwin. Used with permission.

Fluency in Reading

Another constrained skill in reading is fluency, which is defined as the rate and accuracy of oral or silent reading. Students must read smoothly, at a reasonable pace, and with a high degree of accuracy in order to comprehend the text. Reading fluently means that the words are recognized quickly and without extreme effort such that attention to meaning is not undermined. In addition, the reading is performed with prosody, meaning that phrase boundaries, inflection, pauses, and expression accurately reflect what is written. These three components—accuracy, rate of automaticity, and prosody—should be attended to in equal measure (Nichols et al., 2009). Prosody is the patterns of stress and intonation in our language and includes pauses, inflections, and emphasis. Prosody emerges in second or third grade, as students move from what Chall (1983) called "grunting and groaning" to "ungluing from print" (p. 11). Of the three, prosody seems to be the one element most at risk of being overlooked in reading instruction. That is unfortunate, as prosodic readers reflect their understanding of the text they are reading, a proxy for comprehension. Gauging a student's prosody requires listening to him or her read aloud. The good news is that this doesn't need to be accomplished as a separate event. Students read aloud frequently, and it is useful to teach students explicitly about prosody, or "making your reading sound like talking." The National Assessment of Educational Progress (NAEP) prosody scale, developed originally for fourth-grade students, is easy to use and can provide you and the student with a way to discuss prosody (Daane et al., 2005). The prosody scale can be found in Figure 2.8.

Fluency in reading

Prosody seems to be the one element most at risk of being overlooked in reading instruction.

Sixth-grade English teacher Nathan Lomeli meets regularly with a small group of students who are not yet reading at expected levels. At the beginning of the year, Mr. Lomeli taught these students about fluency and prosody in their reading. Using the NAEP holistic rubric as a guide, Mr. Lomeli and his students watched sports reporters deliver news and noted how they used prosody in their reports. This was all for a purpose, of course. Mr. Lomeli is also the coach for several of the school's sports teams. "I told them I wanted to start an in-school podcast to deliver the news of how our teams were doing," he said.

Figure 2.8 National Assessment of Educational Progress Fluency Scale.

Fluent	Level 4	Reads primarily in larger, meaningful phrase groups. Although some regressions, repetitions, and deviations from text may be present, these do not appear to detract from the overall structure of the story. Preservation of the author's syntax is consistent. Some or most of the story is read with expressive interpretation.
Fluent	Level 3	Reads primarily in three- or four-word phrase groups. Some small groupings may be present. However, the majority of phrasing seems appropriate and preserves the syntax of the author. Little or no expressive interpretation is present.
Non-fluent	Level 2	Reads primarily in two-word phrases with some three- or four-word groupings. Some word-by-word reading may be present. Word groupings may seem awkward and unrelated to larger context of sentence or passage.
Non-fluent	Level 1	Reads primarily word-by-word. Occasional two-word or three-word phrases may occur but these are infrequent and/or they do not preserve meaningful syntax.

Source: Daane, M. C., Campbell, J. R., Grigg, W. S., Goodman, M. J., and Oranje, A. (2005). *Fourth-grade students reading aloud: NAEP 2002 special study of oral reading* (NCES 2006-469), p. 28. U.S. Department of Education. Institute of Education Sciences, National Center for Education Statistics. Washington, DC: Government Printing Office.

These students are charged with reporting on a specific sports team and write a short summary each week. They practice the report and record their efforts until they are "ready for airtime." Mr. Lomeli said, "It's actually my way of getting them to engage in repeated reading, which is a solid way to improve reading fluency. It's also a good work habit. You practice what you care about until you get it right."

Reading Fluency Instruction

Mr. Lomeli referred to repeated reading as an effective method for building fluent readers. This instructional technique is just as it sounds, as student read the same passage multiple times in order to increase their rate, accuracy, and prosody. A challenge of repeated reading is to determine when memorization has taken hold, as the technique's effectiveness declines when the student is no longer reading. It's all about eyes on print. Using a language chart of a poem or song that is performed each day becomes less useful over time, as the student moves from reading to recitation.

Another challenge to repeated reading instruction is boredom, a known factor that has a strong negative effect on learning. Hattie's mega-meta-analyses of studies on boredom show an effect size of –0.47, foretelling a profound loss of learning (Hattie Ranking, n. d.). Older students in particular are going to rebel if they don't see any practical reason why they are being asked to read the text multiple times. Build authentic purposes into repeated reading in order to motivate students. The sixth-grade teacher's development of a sports podcast provided his students with a genuine reason to read their copy repeatedly.

Gauging a student's prosody requires listening to the student read aloud.

iStock.com/SolStock

Readers theater is another popular technique for building fluency. This instructional routine requires that students practice a theater-style script together over several days and perform it for their peers (Martinez et al., 1998). The goal is not memorization, and in fact students are required to read the script directly from the page, even in the final performance. No costumes, props, or movement are used. Instead, this is a strictly aural experience for their audience. Fourth-grade teacher Tonya Martino uses readers theater in her social studies class. "We study our state's history," said the teacher. "It's a great opportunity throughout the year for students to enact important historical events. Ms. Martino relies on several sources for her readers theater scripts. Some have been produced by others—"I usually find them on the internet by searching for an historical event and using the keywords *readers theater*," she said. Others are written by the students, and she has kept some of the best examples from past years to use again.

Ms. Martino teaches all the students how to mark their scripts. They use parentheses to mark phrase boundaries, which are strings of words that go together. Students underline twice words or phrases that should be said more loudly or with heightened emotion. Likewise, words or phrases that should be spoken more softly or slowly receive two lines above. "I tell them that it's a reminder to keep the lid on the box," said the teacher. Question and exclamation marks are circled, as are ellipses that signal pauses. Ms. Martino has seen the benefit of this work as the year has progressed. "When I meet them for small group reading instruction, they scan ahead for signals in the text that have to do with vocal delivery," she said. "In addition, we discuss the descriptive tags a writer uses to describe the character's delivery. If it's hesitant, or abrupt, or mirthful, we talk about what that means for reading. Even when you're reading silently, you should be able to hear the voices of the characters in your mind."

Measuring Fluency

Oral reading fluency (ORF) is a curriculum-based measure to gauge progress in reading development. ORF has been used for several decades and is a proven measure for screening purposes as well as for progress monitoring and as a predictor for reading difficulties (Baker et al., 2008). Students read aloud a new passage for one minute, while the teacher notes errors (words read or pronounced incorrectly, read out of order, or omitted; as well as words the student could not identify that were provided by the examiner after a three-second pause) and are compared to a normed table of expected words correct per minute (Hasbrouck & Tindal, 2017; see Figure 2.9). Fifth-grade teacher Tamara Robinson shares the ORF norms with her students to set goals, and with their families as part of her parent-teacher conferences. "I don't want students or families to mindlessly pursue these, so I make sure to cast fluency in the larger context of reading comprehension. I also make sure they understand that these are normed expectations," said Ms. Robinson. "That means the goal is somewhere between 51% and 75%. A goal of 90% might mean that there's less time and attention to other reading goals."

Development of these foundational skills is essential, but not sufficient. In fact, constrained and unconstrained skills develop somewhat independently of one another.

Phonological awareness, alphabetics and phonics, and fluency form the foundation of reading comprehension. As constrained skills, they lend themselves to being counted and are useful for monitoring reading development. However, instruction limited to these dimensions would be unconscionable and would do a huge disservice to students learning to read and reading to learn. Development of these foundational skills is essential, but not sufficient. In fact, constrained and unconstrained skills develop somewhat independently of one another. A large body of research from the cognitive sciences suggests

Figure 2.9 Oral reading fluency norms.

Compiled ORF Norms

Grade	Percentile	Fall WCPM*	Winter WCPM*	Spring WCPM*
1	90		97	116
	75		59	91
	50		29	60
	25		16	34
	10		9	18
2	90	111	131	148
	75	84	109	124
	50	50	84	100
	25	36	59	72
	10	23	35	43
3	90	134	161	166
	75	104	137	139
	50	83	97	112
	25	59	79	91
	10	40	62	63
4	90	153	168	184
	75	125	143	160
	50	94	120	133
	25	75	95	105
	10	60	71	83
5	90	179	183	195
	75	153	160	169
	50	121	133	146
	25	87	109	119
	10	64	84	102
6	90	185	195	204
	75	159	166	173
	50	132	145	146
	25	112	116	122
	10	89	91	91

*WCPM = words correct per minute

Source: Hasbrouck, J. & Tindal, G. (2017). *An update to compiled ORF norms* (Technical report no. 1702), p. 10. Behavioral Research and Teaching, University of Oregon. https://files.eric.ed .gov/fulltext/ED594994.pdf. Used with permission.

that "basic and higher-order skills develop simultaneously and independently rather than sequentially" (Rapp et al., 2007, p. 290). As Tarchi (2015) noted, "Instruction in high-order reading comprehension should be a specific educational target, and treated independently from basic skills instruction" (p. 80). In other words, a focus solely on phonics instruction will not develop background knowledge, for example, and more than the reverse would be true. Careful attention must be paid to both streams of reading development.

Vocabulary in Reading

Vocabulary in reading

Vocabulary knowledge is a strong predictor of reading comprehension (Baumann et al., 2003) and listening comprehension (Gottardo et al., 2018) and as such has a crucial influence on understanding. Vocabulary is considered an unconstrained skill in the sense that it evolves across a lifetime. Consider all the vocabulary you know today that you did not know a decade ago. Your vocabulary will continue to grow because of the reading you will do and the lived experiences and communication opportunities you will have. The oft-quoted statistics about vocabulary knowledge are daunting. Nagy and Anderson estimated that by the time students enter high school, they need to know 88,500 word families (1984). They arrived at this figure by analyzing printed school materials, developing a six-point scale that ranged from semantically transparent to semantically opaque words. *Birdhouse* is quite semantically transparent, while *hogwash* is semantically opaque. *Blueberry* is semantically transparent, while *strawberry* is not. Many word families transcend more than one category. Therefore, knowing the word *inform* can be easily transformed into knowing *informs* and *informed*, but *informant, uninformed* and *disinformation* might prove to be a bit more challenging. However, the majority (about 54,000 word families) contain semantically opaque words, many of which are encountered primarily in reading but not in everyday speech. Semantically opaque words and phrases can be especially confounding for English learners. Doug recalls a middle school student in a meeting about an upcoming overnight school trip who was advised to wear shower sandals to prevent athlete's foot.

"But I would like to have the foot of an athlete," responded this budding soccer player.

For instructional purposes, words are commonly grouped in a hierarchy based on incidence and use. Elementary educators usually discuss words in terms of tiers (Beck et al., 2013). Tier 1 words are terms heard frequently throughout the day and often in spoken language. That last sentence contains a number of Tier 1 words (*words, are, the, day, and, in*). Except for the youngest children, or for those who are new to English, Tier 1 words are not usually explicitly taught. Tier 2 words, on the other hand, are words are more pervasive in written language than in oral language. Many of these are polysemous, meaning they have more than one meaning. For example, take the word *filing*:

- She was <u>filing</u> her nails in an obviously bored manner while the trial dragged on.

- The judge is <u>filing</u> a contempt-of-court charge against her, because as a juror she was supposed to be paying attention.

Tier 3 words are those that have a very specific meaning and are often associated with a particular content area. *Concerto, photosynthesis*, and *polysemous* are examples of Tier 3 words.

Vacca et al. (2017) use a similar scheme to describe vocabulary at the secondary level as general, specialized, and technical vocabulary. See Figure 2.10 for a chart of types of vocabulary.

Which words to teach? It is impossible to directly teach every word or phrase students need, and you wouldn't want to anyway, because they must also learn to solve for unknown words they encounter in their reading. Having said that, some words and phrases should be directly taught. However, previewing a reading and choosing the "hard" words is particularly ineffective, as in practice, selection is intuitive and therefore unreliable in scope. Instead, use a decision-making framework (Frey & Fisher, 2009). The bullet list that follows represents such a framework; it is drawn from the work of Graves and Slater (1996). (See Figure 2.11 for a visual portrait of this decision-making model.)

- *Representative: Is it essential to understand the text?* It is hard to imagine understanding the U.S. Constitution without understanding what the word *constitution* means.

Previewing a reading and choosing the "hard" words is particularly ineffective, as in practice, selection is intuitive and therefore unreliable in scope.

Figure 2.10 Types of vocabulary.

Type	Description	Use	Examples
Tier 1: General/ Everyday	Common in oral and written language Meaning widely agreed on	Everyday speech and high frequency use in print	Barn, cat, girl, happy, them, town, yellow
Tier 2: Specialized/ General Academic	Words with two or more distinct meanings (polysemic), and words used differently across content or subjects	Contextual use shapes the meaning and sometimes the pronunciation of the word	Bias, blue, calibrate, establish, firm, incidental, note, setting, subject, verify, wash
Tier 3: Technical/ Domain Specific	Low-frequency words with a distinctive meaning and associated with one content or subject area	Primarily used in text and spoken in highly contextualized environments (e.g., a lecture or classroom)	Alliteration, calligraphy, cardiac, entomologist, isotope, octave, solar, sonnet, system, totalitarianism

- *Repeatability: Will this word be used again in this text or course?* If the answer is yes, it may be worth teaching directly. However, hold off until you consider later questions about contextual and structural analysis.

- *Transportable: Can this be used in other subjects?* Specialized vocabulary words are often orphaned because no one discipline owns them. Yet words like *analyze, distinguish*, and *simplify* have high utility across applications.

- *Contextual analysis: Can students arrive at the meaning through context?* If the answer is yes, this is a great word-solving opportunity that shouldn't be wasted through direct instruction. Have students apply their knowledge to arrive at a meaning.

- *Structural analysis: Can students arrive at meaning through structure?* Morphological analysis (units of meaning) can unlock some words, especially those with Latin or Greek roots. *Mediterranean Sea* is a great one for middle school students to take apart, as *medi-* means middle, and *terra* refers to land. Understanding that this ancient sea was in the middle of the land known to inhabitants of the region deepens meaning.

- *Cognitive load: How many words are reasonable to teach?* A judgment call, to be sure, and one that is impacted by students' developmental levels. However, two to five words for a short reading to be consumed in one lesson is probably enough.

Direct and Intentional Vocabulary Instruction

Once targeted words have been selected, develop a reliable routine for teaching them. Words that are directly taught should not hijack the reading but instead should illuminate it. We like the routine developed by Tennyson and Cocchiarella (1986). We'll use the word *analyze* to demonstrate.

1. *Label and define.* Students first need to be able to attach a short meaning and a label to an unfamiliar word. The teacher might pause to say, "Analyze means to look at something carefully so you can solve a problem."

Figure 2.11 **A decision-making model for selected targeted vocabulary words and phrases.**

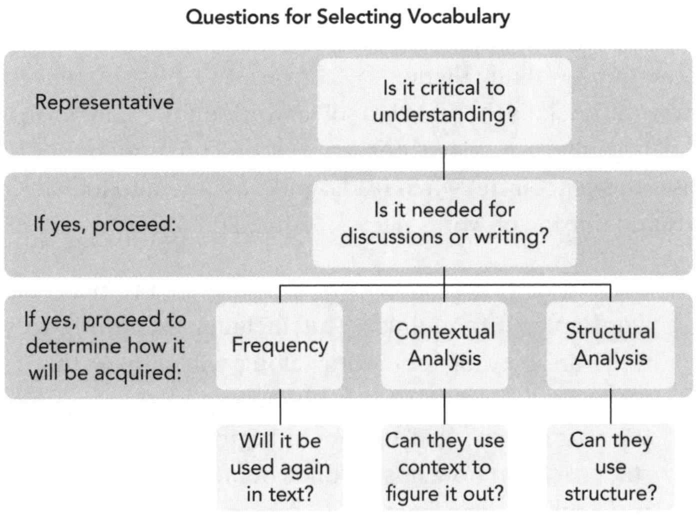

Questions for Selecting Vocabulary

Representative	Is it critical to understanding?	
If yes, proceed:	Is it needed for discussions or writing?	
If yes, proceed to determine how it will be acquired:	Frequency — Contextual Analysis — Structural Analysis	
	Will it be used again in text? — Can they use context to figure it out? — Can they use structure?	

Source: Visible Learning for Literacy Surface Learning Workshop, slide 69. 2017 © Corwin. Used with permission.

2. *Contextualize.* After defining, ground the word or phrase within the author's use. "I'm going to reread that sentence now. 'The police detective analyzed the crime scene for clues.' Since *analyze* means to look closely to solve a problem, I know he's trying to figure out what happened."

3. *Give a best example.* Link the word to something they might already know. "Some of you have told me about you use Fortnite analysis videos on YouTube to improve your online gaming skills. You're not just watching. You're solving problems to get better at the game."

4. *Elaborate on attributes.* Contrastive examples help students understand what it is *not.* "When someone is analyzing something, they're breaking it apart into smaller pieces so they can look more closely to understand. A police detective that wasn't looking carefully wouldn't be able to analyze the scene."

5. *Provide strategy information.* Tell students a strategy you used to figure out the word. "I've heard this word used before on other TV crime shows. So, I thought about how it was used and then made a connection to the story we're reading now."

Teaching Word Solving

You must equip students with the skills they need to solve words on their own. We teach our own students a system for figuring out unfamiliar words and phrases they encounter when reading.

You can't be a walking dictionary for your students; you must equip them with the skills they need to solve words on their own. We teach our own students a system for figuring out unfamiliar words and phrases they encounter when reading. We ask them to look inside of words and outside of words (Frey & Fisher, 2009).

1. *Look inside the word for structural clues.* Can you break the word apart into chunks? This includes examining to see if there are base or root words along with affixes that reveal further meaning. In addition, you may be able to determine the part of speech. This should begin in the early grades as students learn how smaller units of meaning are combined to make multisyllabic words.

2. *Look outside the word or phrase for contextual clues.* Not all words can be analyzed structurally, but sometimes the author will give you a definition or a synonym that reveals the meaning. A sentence that reads "The house was cozy, and the people inside were <u>warm</u> and <u>safe</u>" offers context clues to unlock the meaning of *cozy*. Contextual clues come in several forms:

   - *Look for antonym or contrast clues.* A word or phrase is clarified using an opposite meaning. "She was <u>brave</u> as she faced her enemy. She would not run away and be called a coward."

   - *Look for a restatement or synonym clue.* The word or phrase is restated using more common terms. "The police detective discovered that the security guard <u>shirked</u> his duty. The jewelry store was left unprotected when the guard departed before his shift was over."

   - *Look for a definition or example clue.* The word or phrase is defined within the sentence. "The science of <u>physiology</u> is the study of how bodies move and function."

3. *When structural and contextual analysis fails, look further outside the word or phrase.* This is when resources should be utilized: dictionaries, glossaries, a quick internet search. Even asking another person is acceptable.

Four Principles for Vocabulary Instruction

What are the unexpected benefits of spending thousands of hours observing vocabulary instruction? A team of researchers found out during a three-year intensive study of vocabulary instruction in middle grades classrooms (Manyak et al., 2014). The focus of their work was developing and revising solid practices for teaching targeted vocabulary words. In the process of their research, they noticed that several principles of effective instructional practice emerged. The researchers and several of the teachers involved in the project went back through their data to perform a qualitative analysis of the interactions between teachers and students and their vocabulary learning. They identified four principles that apply across a range of classrooms, subject areas, and students (see Figure 2.12).

Figure 2.12 Four pragmatic principles for enhancing vocabulary instruction.

1. Establish efficient yet rich routines for introducing target words.

Intensive, multifaceted vocabulary instruction can take a significant amount of instructional time. Thus, efficient, rich routines for introducing word meanings are critical when teaching a large number of target words.

2. Provide review experiences that promote deep processing of target words.

In addition to benefiting from efficiency in target word instruction, students benefit from active and deep processing of word meanings. Ongoing review should be used to provide students with multiple exposures to target words and to promote deep processing.

3. Respond directly to student confusion by using anchor experiences.

Students can easily become confused when learning new word meanings. Such confusion can spread from student to student, and teachers should thus respond directly to inaccurate usages by providing students with clear anchor definitions and examples.

4. Foster universal participation and accountability.

Students with greater vocabulary knowledge can dominate word-meaning instruction, causing other students to become passive. Therefore, it is important to foster universal participation in vocabulary activities and to hold all students accountable for learning word meanings.

Source: Manyak, P. C., Gunten, H. V., Autenrieth, D., Gillis, C., Mastre-O'Farrell, J., Irvine-McDermott, E., Baumann, J. F., & Blachowicz, C. L. Z. (2014). Four practical principles for enhancing vocabulary instruction, p. 16. *The Reading Teacher, 68*(1), 13–23.

The Importance of Routines

The first principle relates to the *importance of routines* for introducing targeted vocabulary. Teachers in the project did not all use the same routine. Instead, the importance was in having a routine and sticking with it so that students could become habituated to how words and phrases were initially profiled. For instance, ninth-grade English teacher Holly Iverson has developed her own routine and consistently applies it. She introduces targeted words in the context of the text, provides a definition, and models several examples. When Ms. Iverson introduced the word *disparate* in the context of its use in Quindlen's article, "A Quilt of a Country" (2001), a piece written two weeks after the 9/11 attacks, she said,

> Let me show you a word that's important for this article we're going to read. It's *disparate*. Listen to this

sentence: "Once these disparate ideas were held together by a common enemy, by the fault lines of world wars and the electrified fence of communism." Disparate means things that are so different from each other they can't be compared. Like the phrase "apples and oranges" means they are so different you can't compare them. When ideas are disparate, which is what she's referring to, it means the ideas are so unlike that they just can't seem to go together at all.

The teacher then shows a photo of a man wearing a plaid jacket, striped pants, and a flowered shirt. "This is the fashion version of *disparate*," she laughs. "It just doesn't go together!" She then solicits a few examples from the class, who offer some unlikely celebrity couplings. One talks about the phrase "oil and water," and another offers, "A blow dryer and a sink full of water are disparate for sure!"

What's most important is that the routine she uses engages in several dimensions of instruction, including direct instruction, modeling, teaching with examples, and inviting students to discuss ideas from their own lives. Moreover, this routine takes about five minutes of time and does not distract from the lesson at hand, which is to read and discuss the article.

Ongoing Review

A second principle identified by the researchers was *ongoing review* to deepen vocabulary learning (Manyak et al., 2014). Initial introduction of targeted words and phrases isn't sufficient for deep learning. Instead, students need repeated exposure in order to enrich their schema. After all, vocabulary instruction should not be limited to definitional meaning. Rather, these words and phrases represent complex concepts. An essential dimension of word knowledge is understanding the relationships between terms.

Second-grade teacher Lydia Tomás uses short activities such as Connect Two, an activity profiled by the researchers, with her vocabulary word wall. "The word wall features terms we are currently learning as well as those from previous units," said the teacher. Several times a week she leads the class in games using the word wall. Connect Two is a challenging one, as student teams work to pair a current word with one learned in an earlier unit of study. The teams' challenge is to then explain the connection. "Sometimes I give them the two words, and other times I name the connection," explained Ms. Tomás. "They come up with the missing part of the equation."

Current words from their science unit are highlighted in this lesson. "I'm going to use a current word—*characteristics*—and an old word—*feature*. What's the connection?" Students talk among themselves about ideas, and Inelda raises her hand on behalf of her group.

"We think characteristics and features are connected because they mean almost the same thing. It's like a . . . a sin . . . I forget the word."

Ms. Tomás nods. "A synonym, right? Two words that are similar. Thanks for that, you're right. So the next challenge is to find another synonym pair using a current science word and another word on the word wall." Several groups identify pairings, including *record* and *observe*, *direction* and *rule*, and *appearance* and *trait*; and they explain their thinking.

"That's the most valuable part," the teacher remarked later. "I get to hear their reasoning and their use of academic language."

Responding Directly When Confusions Are in Evidence

A third principle of robust vocabulary instruction is *responding directly when confusions are in evidence* (Manyak et al., 2014). Vocabulary learning is incremental as schema are built, and words and phrases that are new to students are likely to be only partially understood. This is particularly true when the term represents an abstract concept. When it is evident that understanding is incomplete, the teacher should respond by redefining the word and providing an anchoring experience that includes new examples. This happened during a teacher-led small group discussion of an informational text about Dr. Martin Luther King Jr. Fifth-grade teacher Ruben Wasserman's students read that the civil rights leader was a "dynamic speaker." But Jacob, one of four students meeting with Mr. Wasserman, had a puzzled look on his face. "Um . . . so he changed all the time in his speeches?" asked the boy. When asked to explain why he thought so, Jacob said, "Well, he's like a dynamic character, right?" The teacher recognized his student's confusion. "I can see why you thought that," responded Mr. Wasserman.

You're thinking about a literary term we learned a few weeks ago—a *dynamic character*. That's a description of a character who changes over the course of the story. You'll remember that the opposite of a dynamic character is a flat character. The word *dynamic* is what's throwing you in this case. When the author describes King as a dynamic speaker, it means that he is energetic and inspiring to his audience. A dynamic speaker's not a boring one. Let's look for evidence in this paragraph that Dr. King was an energetic and inspiring speaker—a *dynamic* speaker. Isaac, Rebekah, and Ruth, I want each of you to find evidence, too. When you've located it, put your finger on it so I can see you've found it.

Fostering Universal Participation and Accountability

By inviting the other three students into the discussion, Mr. Wasserman is enacting the fourth principle, *fostering universal participation and accountability*. The teacher knows that one of the students is often quicker to answer before the others. He wants to make sure that all his students in the group are attending to the discussion and reexamining the text.

"Their silent signal lets me know they're following along. Because it's a small group, I can rapidly determine who has it and who doesn't," explained Mr. Wasserman. "It's one way I'm checking for understanding."

Without question, vocabulary is an essential reading comprehension skill, but one that is diminished when instruction isn't aligned with best practices. To teach vocabulary as a definitional list of words to be memorized thwarts schema development. To choose words for direct instruction based on intuition alone results in gaps that undermine understanding. And to fail to equip students with problem-solving tools to determine the meaning of unknown words and phrases robs them of the confidence they need to read complex texts. As an unconstrained skill, a person's vocabulary must continue to grow over a lifetime. Likewise, the final reading comprehension skill we address in this chapter is *knowledge*, widely understood as a solid predictor of text comprehension (e.g., Alexander & Jetton, 2000; McNamara & Kintsch, 1996).

> To teach vocabulary as a definitional list of words to be memorized thwarts schema development.

Comprehension Strategy Instruction

In terms of comprehension skills specifically, Block and Lacina (2009) suggest that there are more than 30 cognitive and metacognitive processes that readers use (see Figure 2.13). Highly proficient readers who deeply understand the texts they read have likely reached automaticity with each of these processes. Importantly, automaticity takes practice. Yes, students need to be introduced to strategies, and then they need practice and feedback to transition these into skills.

Teacher modeling using a think-aloud process is an effective instructional approach for developing students' skills. Teachers verbalize their expert thinking such that students can imitate similar cognitive

> Students need to be introduced to strategies, and then they need practice and feedback to transition these into skills.

Figure 2.13 Cognitive and metacognitive processes for comprehending texts.

Making connections to background knowledge	Recognizing personal perspective
Interpreting text structures	Identifying gists
Questioning	Changing hypotheses
Clarifying meaning	Adding hypotheses
Comparing	Searching for meaning
Contrasting	Being alert to main ideas
Summarizing	Creating themes
Imaging	Determining importance
Setting purposes	Drawing inferences
Using fix-up strategies	Corroborating congenial and noncongenial data
Monitoring	Contextualizing
Cognizing	Engaging in retrospection
Interpreting authors' intentions	Generating and using mnemonic devices
Pausing to reflect	
Paraphrasing	Predicting
Analyzing	Organizing and reorganizing text

Source: Block, C. C., & Lacina, J. (2009). Comprehension instruction in kindergarten through grade three. In S. E. Israel & G. G. Duffy (Eds.), *Handbook of research on reading comprehension* (pp. 494–509). Routledge.

and metacognitive actions. It is an apprenticeship technique in which students learn to approximate the actions of another, more skilled person. For example, a teacher might say,

> I've noticed that I'm not really understanding this para-graph. I think that I'll go back to reread, because it might be that I lost focus and wasn't paying attention. If that doesn't work, then I think I'll focus on the words that are confusing to me.

The teacher then proceeds to demonstrate exactly that as students observe. In turn, they apply these same strategies to similarly complex text in order to support their own understanding. Each of the aspects of comprehension identified by Block and Lacina (2009) can be taught through modeling. Importantly, teachers need to model regularly for students. It's an apprenticeship approach, slowly building habits that students will begin to deploy automatically. A few examples follow.

Inferring

Understanding implied messages is critical for comprehension. Authors do not state everything explicitly and instead rely on the reader to supply information and draw conclusions based on what is known. Inferences occur "when the reader activates information that is evoked by, yet goes beyond, the information that is provided explicitly in the text" (Van den Broek et al., 1993, p. 170). Sometimes referred to as "reading between the lines" or a blending of "text-based connections and schema-based connections" (Herber, 1978, p. 154), inferring is a complex cognitive process that can easily go astray.

Modeling inferring, especially with highly visual sequential art, can help students build this habit and apply it to increasingly complex pieces of text.

Graphic novels can be especially useful in modeling elaborative inferences. The space between the panels is called the gutter, and it is the place where the reader must make inferences (McCloud, 1994). There are any number of graphic novels you can use to introduce students to making inferences. For example, Nancy likes to use a single page from Will Eisner's book *New York: The Big City* (2000) (see Figure 2.14). As with her students, our understanding of this page is based on our ability to infer. Do you think that the two people are in an argument in the first few panels? If so, how do you know? Nancy likes to imagine (infer) that the man is apologizing in Panel 5. If you made a similar inference, did you infer that they made up? Interestingly, from the worm's eye view, you can make a number of inferences about what's happening on the street. This is what readers have to do all of the time. Modeling inferring, especially with highly visual sequential art, can help students build this habit and apply it to increasingly complex pieces of text.

Figure 2.14 Worm's eye view graphic novel.

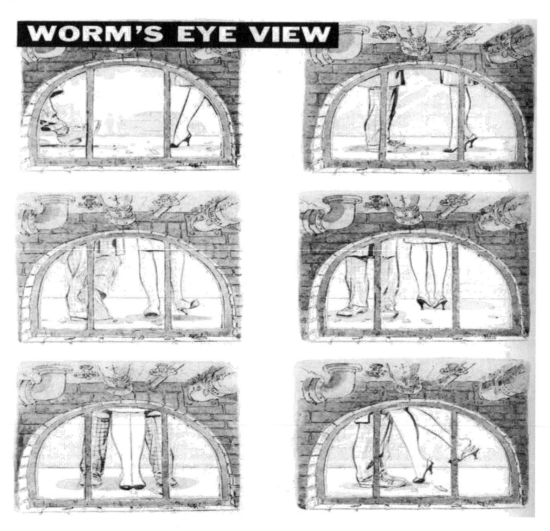

Source: Worm's Eye View (Page 102)." Copyright © 1981, 1982, 1983, 1986 by Will Eisner. Copyright © 2006 by the Estate of Will Eisner, from WILL EISNER'S NEW YORK: LIFE IN THE BIG CITY by Will Eisner. Used by permission of W. W. Norton & Company, Inc.

Summarizing and Synthesizing

Readers cannot remember everything that they read; the cognitive load is simply too heavy. Instead, readers have to remember salient points and key ideas. The word *summarize* means to

- Present the substance or general idea in brief form

- Create a concise, condensed account of the original

- Cover the main points

Summarizing improves students' reading comprehension of fiction and nonfiction alike, as it helps the reader construct an *overall* understanding of a text (Rinehart et al., 1986). When summarizing, students focus on the gist of the reading, not the trivia or details. Some clues that students find helpful as they develop quality summaries include the following:

- Specifics from the title

- Information at the beginning of the selection

- Questions that the author asks or implies

- Surprises or revelations

- Information presented in tables or figures

- Details that are repeated

- Headings, subheads, and italicized text

- Changes in character, tone, mood, setting, plot

- Data provided at the end of the selection

Ms. Jenkins modeled summarizing and synthesizing after reading a text selection about genetic variation. The text contained lots of details and was very interesting. The margin notes contained bits of information that captured the readers' interest. As Ms. Jenkins noted after reading aloud the text and modeling along the way,

> Wow, that's a lot to remember! I'm going to take a minute right now and summarize what I remember. The notes on the side of the text about eye color were exceptionally

interesting. Do you remember that? Talk with a partner about the ways in which eye color is carried from one generation to the next.

The students in this biology class quickly turned to one another and began talking. Nicole said to Josiah, "The grandparents had different colored eyes; one blue and one brown. But the brown ones are dominant, so all of their children had brown eyes, but had the recessive gene for blue eyes." The conversation continued for a few minutes, until Ms. Jenkins began speaking again.

Yes, inherited eye color is very interesting, but it's not the main point of the selection. I know that the author was trying to provide me with an example, but I need to remember the major points. One major point that I'd like to summarize is that genes contain the instructions needed in order to construct a human body, and that variation in the code produces individual differences. Can you summarize another major point with a partner? Then we'll collect the major points and create our synthesis.

Her summary provided students with an example of the type of thinking required of the task. She also invited students into the process, as they discussed major points with a partner. Using her example, students identified key ideas from the reading, and the resulting summary included the main ideas. Along the way, students gained a valuable experience—they learned how to summarize and were not simply told to summarize.

Monitoring

Comprehension monitoring is the capacity of a reader to notice while reading whether a text is making sense or not. Monitoring is a habit for effective readers; we tend to know right away when a text is not making sense. Most readers have had the experience of reading along and suddenly realizing that they have no idea what they just read. This may be because they are tired (reading too late at night in bed, for example) or because the text is simply too difficult. In addition, the reader might have encountered some of the following (e.g., McKeown & Gentilucci, 2007; Yang, 2006):

- New words or known words that do not make sense in context

- Sentences that are vague, ambiguous, or inconsistent with background knowledge

- Paragraphs in which relationships are unclear, conflicting, or connected in several possible ways

The difference between skilled and struggling readers is in what they do when comprehension is compromised. Skilled readers do not simply notice that they have lost the meaning. They also have plans for fixing up their comprehension.

Mr. Hargrove models monitoring for his students as a component of each reading he does. As he reads aloud, he regularly makes comments about whether or not the text makes sense. Naturally, he models a number of other comprehension strategies in each reading, too. For example, while reading the text of George Washington's farewell address (1796), Mr. Hargrove notes that the first sentence was a bit confusing. Washington's first paragraph reads,

> Friends and Fellow Citizens:
>
> The period for a new election of a citizen to administer the executive government of the United States being not far distant, and the time actually arrived when your thoughts must be employed in designating the person who is to be clothed with that important trust, it appears to me proper, especially as it may conduce to a more distinct expression of the public voice, that I should now apprise you of the resolution I have formed, to decline being considered among the number of those out of whom a choice is to be made.

Mr. Hargrove says, "I'll have to reread this, as I noticed that I got a little lost in what he was saying." He reads aloud the passage again.

> I have to make some connections here. Washington is talking about the presidency but is using different language—he never actually says, "president." It's true that the president is a citizen who administers the executive

The difference between skilled and struggling readers is in what they do when comprehension is compromised.

branch of the United States government, but when he first said it that way, I wasn't sure what he was saying.

Mr. Hargrove knows that this serves to remind his students about the importance of monitoring comprehension.

Of course, we could go on, but suffice it to say that students need to be introduced to comprehension strategies by their teachers, and they need to be taught when, why, and how to use them. In addition, students need practice with these strategies to develop automaticity. Of course, as we will explore in the final chapter of this book, the complexity of the text will impact students' ability to deploy their skills and strategies.

Students need to be introduced to comprehension strategies by their teachers, and they need to be taught when, why, and how to use them.

Conclusion

There are many skills that contribute to text comprehension. These skills must be taught and practiced if students are to become independent and proficient readers. In this chapter, we focused on the ways in which teachers can enable students to develop the necessary skills required for them to comprehend. But as texts change, the skills can be challenged, and comprehension can be lost. Students need practice with a wide range of texts if they are to generalize their skills. Having said that, skill instruction is not enough to ensure that students understand what they read. Without attention to the *will* and *thrill* of comprehension, reading becomes a passive and compliance-oriented experience. In those cases, students are dragged through texts, and they can sometimes apply the skills that they have been taught. But they do not engage with reading, nor do they see reading as a valuable asset that they can use to impact the world. Deep comprehension requires that students develop the skills required to understand what they read as well as the will and thrill of doing so.

Will in Reading Comprehension

Tenth-grade English teacher Felice Harrison has two very different readers in the same classroom. One student, Nyah, is by every measure a strong and avid reader. Reading comprehension assessments show her to exceed grade-level expectations, and her disposition toward reading mirrors her advanced skill set. After Nyah read a review on a website about *Red at the Bone*, a new novel for adults written by Jacqueline Woodson (2019), she couldn't wait to get her hands on it. She told Ms. Harrison about the review and said, "She's been one of my favorite authors since I was little. She gets me."

Nyah rattled off a list of Woodson's previous works and then said, "Could I start a book club for this book? I've got friends I know would love this. We could meet at lunch in your room. And you could be a part of it." Nyah is every teacher's dream—a self-starter and a voracious reader with a high degree of agency about getting things done.

Kamile is also in Ms. Harrison's class. Unlike Nyah, Kamile avoids reading and has commented, "I like [Ms. Harrison] but I hate English." According to a variety of reading assessments, Kamile reads well below grade level. Ms. Harrison knows that motivation plays a significant role in reading, especially for adolescents. A few weeks earlier, she introduced Kamile to another author, Nikki Grimes.

"I keep some of my personal favorites here," she said, gesturing to the small bookcase near her desk. The teacher scanned the shelves and pulled out three titles, including *Bronx Masquerade* (Grimes, 2002).

Ms. Harrison briefly described each, but Kamile was drawn to the story of 19 high school students, told through prose and poetry. "It reminds me of that movie my aunt loves, *The Breakfast Club."*

Ms. Harrison laughed. "Now that's an interesting thought," she said. "How about you try it and we'll talk again in a few days. I'd love to hear what you think of it."

The book has a quantitative text complexity level similar to Kamile's current reading level but is qualitatively more complex, with lots of figurative language in the poetry portions. The teacher suspects that Kamile's background knowledge and interest balance this out, and that the book will stretch Kamile's skills while capitalizing on her motivation. Ms. Harrison also understands that finding an enjoyable author can encourage a reluctant reader to try another book.

Ms. Harrison keeps a copy of another book, *Bird by Bird: Some Instructions on Writing and Life*, on that shelf. When asked later about her own approach to matching readers and books, she turned to a passage in the well-worn book and read aloud the words of Anne Lamott,

> For some of us, books are as important as almost anything else on earth. What a miracle it is that out of these small, flat, rigid squares of paper unfolds world after world after world, worlds that sing to you, comfort and quiet or excite you. Books help us understand who we are and how we are to behave. They show us what community and friendship mean; they show us how to live and die. (1995, p. 13)

"For me, that's what reading is all about," Ms. Harrison later remarked. "It's how we build communities and how we understand ourselves in the context of our communities. Nyah and Kamile have a community in books just waiting for them." The difference is that students like Nyah have found that community, on the page and in the conversations she has with others. Kamile hasn't found it yet but has the potential to do so. Her interest, even in the presence of lower reading skills relative to her age, can spark a higher volume of voluntary reading.

Ms. Harrison's view of her readers is borne out in recent evidence about voluntary reading habits. Researchers conducted a unique longitudinal study of 2,525 students' leisure reading habits from first grade through ninth grade. They were interested in examining the relationship between voluntary reading outside of school and the reading ability of students. Previous studies have demonstrated that there is a correlation between out-of-school reading and reading competence (e.g., Anderson et al., 1988). But this group wanted to get closer to causation. Their question: Does more reading make for stronger readers, or do stronger readers engage in more reading? It is a bit of a chicken-and-egg question in that the relationship between voluntary reading and reading competence has been unclear.

They found that the habit of voluntary reading among young readers (those in grades K–2) is influenced by the child's ability to decode fluently. However, the influence of decoding fluency (a constrained skill) decreases as automatic recognition of letter patterns consolidates. After the early grades, reading comprehension, regardless of the skill level, has a stronger influence on whether a student will engage (or not) in volitional reading (Torppa et al., 2019). Noting that "in the later grades . . . active book reading in particular was reciprocally associated with reading comprehension but not with reading fluency," the researchers concluded that reading interest and not relative skill made the difference. The researchers concluded,

> It is also crucial to recognize that will is not a static characteristic—either you have it or you don't—but rather an influence that we as teachers can actively impact.

> We should pay close attention to the development of reading interest from early grades onwards. This is particularly important for the poorest readers who are at particular risk for not developing a positive attitude to reading when poor skills hamper the interest in leisure reading during the early grades. (p. 15)

Older readers, even those who possess reading skills below grade level, can be motivated to engage with more voluntary reading. Ms. Harrison draws on what Worthy and colleagues call "the human factor in reaching resistant readers" (2002, p. 177). The social interactions between her and Kamile, especially in the teacher's invitation into a community of readers, can be of great importance for students who don't seek out reading on their own. The willingness to invest extra time and effort in a student rests at the core of what effective teachers do. As fortunate as we are to have students like Nyah, our collective responsibility is to build the will of students like Kamile. Students need comprehension skills, which should be taught systematically and with the goal of mastery of increasingly challenging texts. But skill alone is insufficient for sustaining effort. The will; which is to say the desire, motivation, and habits of reading; are crucial in the development of reading comprehension. Even the best-developed skills will deteriorate over time if they are not regularly used. Having said that, it is also crucial to recognize that will is not a static characteristic—either you have it or you don't—but rather an influence that we as teachers can actively impact. This chapter is about the essential role of will in reading comprehension, and the many ways we can incubate reader dispositions with an eye toward building and sustaining motivation.

Will in Reading Comprehension

Learning is driven by an internal desire to learn. These desires are sometimes goal directed, such as preparing to compete in one's first 10K race, or learning the basics of a new language in anticipation of an international trip. At other times, the reason may be less obvious. You might want to learn more about comic book superheroes because there seems to be an endless stream of movies about them, and even though you're not especially interested, you'd like to be able to hold your own in casual conversations. Or perhaps you've been through an especially rough patch personally, and you need to incorporate some new self-care habits in life to regain equilibrium. These motivations vary depending on the circumstances, yet they are also universal across people.

The "will to read"

Motivations for learning are influenced by dispositions toward learning. One's approach to learning is a life skill, not just one used at school. The metaphor of a river of learning is useful in understanding the interplay among knowledge, skills, and dispositions (Claxton, 2018). As seen in Figure 3.1, the surface of a river is much like knowledge in school—it runs fast, and it is easily seen by teachers and students. Just below the surface are the literacies needed to acquire knowledge, especially reading, writing, and numeracy. These are a bit less apparent, as they are the undercurrent and are therefore more challenging to measure and track. The deepest layer is also the least apparent to either the teacher or the learner. The dispositions and attitudes toward learning—such as tolerance for errors, a willingness to embrace challenge, and the emotional strength to persevere—influence the learning that occurs at the surface. Importantly, not all high-achieving students possess these dispositions, any more than those not yet making expected progress lack them.

The dispositions toward reading, or what we call *will*, must be taught with the same intention and vigor as the skills of reading comprehension. There is good reason to do so, as reading comprehension growth is associated with reading motivation (Guthrie et al., 2007). Further, students' attitudes toward reading mediate teachers' instructional influence (Huang & Chen 2019). In other words, student reading attitudes impact instructional benefit. In their study of nearly 4,000 fourth-grade students, researchers found that the effectiveness of a teacher's reading comprehension skills instruction was dependent to a significant degree on the students' attitude toward reading. Students with a negative attitude did not benefit as much from the teacher's instruction, regardless of their reading skills level.

Figure 3.1 The learning river.

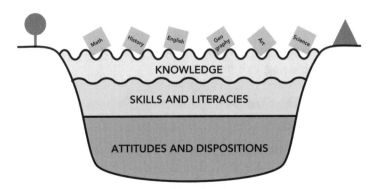

Source: Claxton, G. (2017). *The learning power approach: Teaching learners to teach themselves.* Thousand Oaks, CA: Corwin, 2017. Used with permission of Juan and Becky Carlzon.

Students' attitudes toward reading mediate teachers' instructional influence.

The four dimensions of dispositions for learning

Children's self-concept as readers begins in the primary grades and has a reciprocal relationship to their level of reading fluency (Quirk et al., 2009). Second-grade students were followed for a year and assessed three times on measures of reading fluency and on the Motivation to Read Profile (MRP; Gambrell et al., 1996). The MRP asks students to respond to items such as "Knowing how to read is (very important/not important)" and "I worry about what other kids think of my reading (every day/never)." The researchers found that students who possessed a low reading self-concept were less fluent readers, and that this relationship persisted across the school year. This is consistent with other research that low reading self-concept begins as early as the end of first grade (Chapman & Tunmer, 2003). While it was once believed that young children did not acquire a negative self-concept as learners until the intermediate grades, newer research on primary students has shown that reading attitudes develop much earlier. The result can be devastating, as young children who do not see themselves as readers will avoid it as much as possible. Adolescents like Kamile who "hate reading" begin their school careers as emergent readers who face difficulty breaking the code. Even after they have done so, the negative effects of low self-concept, combined with similarly negative attitudes and dispositions about reading, can linger.

Dispositions That Underpin Learning

If skill were all that stood between us and a better life, things would be a lot easier. Unfortunately, that isn't human nature. Our dispositions influence the decisions we make every day and are separate from our ability to execute a skill. We may have the ability to exercise, for instance, but lack the disposition to do so regularly. Likewise, students may have the ability to read but choose not to. Thus, they are aliterate. Dispositions toward learning impact the degree to which we persist when a task is challenging, as well as whether we believe we can be successful and whether we seek help when it is needed.

The desire to read has a powerful impact on learning to read, and its roots are in early experiences. Neuman et al. (2000) write,

> Beginning in infancy and continuing throughout childhood, children may learn from those around them that in language and literacy there is value, enjoyment, and sheer power. If they do not develop such an interest in reading and writing—an eager desire for initiation into print's mysteries and skills— children's progress toward literacy is uncertain. When the going gets tough, they may drop out of the game. While eagerness does not guarantee success, motivated children are far more likely to persist and succeed than are children who see no point in all the hard work of learning to read and write. (p. 28)

The desire to read—what we call the will to read—can foreshadow a student's academic trajectory. Consider two students in Karen McCall's third-grade class. Mateo's learning dispositions are clearly strong and positive. He seeks out complex books that will challenge his knowledge, keeps his own list of books he has read, and is eager to talk with others about what he is reading. Alvaro, on the other hand, possesses dispositions toward reading that are avoidant. He will read when he is required to do so, but no more than that. When asked to select a passage to read, he invariably chooses based on length, the shorter the better. Alvaro abandons books regularly. "I think he's read the first five pages of most of the books in my class library," said Ms. McCall. Yet on quantitative and qualitative reading measures, the boys score similarly, comfortably in the range of grade-level expectations. The difference is in their dispositions, or what Claxton (2017) calls their learning power. These capacities for life-long learning, which is to say self-sustaining learning, foretell one's informal learning possibilities outside of the classroom.

Five years later, both of the boys are now in eighth grade. Mateo has made knowledge gains, fueled by curiosities about subjects of interest to him. He is learning about coding and has recently started making beats with a software program. "I even sold two!" he announced, a budding entrepreneur. Not surprisingly, his reading list is skewed toward these topics. Alvaro is lagging further behind and is now reading two grade levels below expectations. "He drifts," remarked Scott Fraser, his English teacher. "He's one of those hard-to-reach kids for me. I'm still looking for ways to light a fire in him." Their relative learning power, or dispositions, are impacted by the 4R's: resilience, resourcefulness, reflection, and relating (Claxton, 2017). These are not learning behaviors, but rather learning habits and tendencies. They carry with them the potential for students to be active learners in and out of school. Without these dispositions, the potential to learn is diminished.

Resilience: Emotional Strength

All learning has an emotional dimension, and the disposition of resilience speaks to persistence, but also to the emotional engagement or flow of the learning. When caught in the flow, one's attention and ability to concentrate, while screening out distractions, is heightened. It is an optimal experience that transcends time and space. Flow is the just-right balance between challenge and skill—not too hard, not too boring (Csikszentmihalyi, 2008; see Figure 3.2). Of course, no one can sustain an optimal level of experience at all times, but it is a worthy target to create as often as possible for students. Note that tasks that are too challenging relative to one's skill level induce anxiety, while tasks that are too simple for a person with a higher degree of skills cause boredom. To be sure, these are definitely emotional states that we as teachers seek to avoid!

Readers talk about "getting lost in a book," and there is evidence that students who experienced this during reading usually had a hand in selecting the text. Having said that, students reported that flow also occurred during assigned readings if the topic was of interest (Mcquillan & Conde, 1996). Importantly, students, especially young ones, benefit from feeling successful in their own independent reading. Younger, less skilled readers who are necessarily reading more laboriously and at slower rates may not experience the same enjoyment or competence in everything they read (Becker et al., 2010). Many primary teachers have discovered the motivating power of having familiar books freely available for their students to read again and again. Feelings of accomplishment build students' reservoir of competence to take on more challenging texts.

Figure 3.2 Flow as the relationship between challenge and skill.

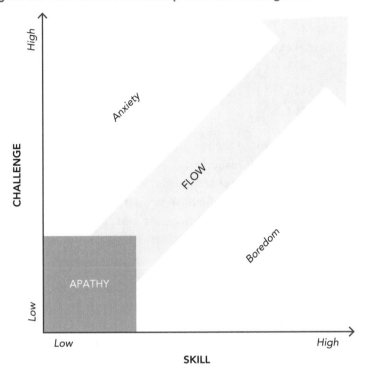

Resourcefulness: Cognitive Capacity

A second dimension of learning dispositions concerns the resourcefulness of the student to leverage skills to make things work. Some of these are related directly to reading comprehension skills, such as formulating questions and making connections to other knowledge, subjects, and texts. However, another element of resourcefulness is reasoning. In reading, reasoning is a function of drawing inferences. When reading narrative texts, the ability to infer a character's motivation, for example, requires being able to deduce how circumstances might logically influence the character's actions. When reading informational texts, reasoning is used to deduce whether the writer's argument is sound and valid. For instance, a reader uses reasoning when she recognizes that just because an author has stated several pieces of evidence to support his claim, it doesn't mean that there isn't other evidence to refute the claim. Reasoning works at the microlevel of the text, too. The relative cohesion of a text—how concepts and ideas hang together—make a text more or less complex. Consider these two possible sentences in an elementary science text (as quoted in Millis et al., 2013, p. 225):

- One part of the cloud develops a downdraft. Rain begins to fall.

- One part of the cloud develops a downdraft, which causes rain to fall.

Advanced readers would see no difference cognitively between the two. However, a young reader with fewer reasoning skills needs the essential word *which* in the second sentence. The word serves as a bridge a reader would otherwise have to infer, which is the cause and effect relationship between a downdraft and the rain. *Which* does the reasoning work for the third grader, who might be reading the sentence in a passage about weather.

Reasoning takes on an increasingly important role in predicting reading comprehension across the school years. In third grade, the most dominant predictor of reading comprehension is fluency. But by seventh grade, reasoning and fluency serve as copredictors of reading comprehension. By tenth grade, it is reasoning alone that is predictive (Tighe & Schatschneider, 2014). This may be due in part to the fact that school texts written for older students do not contain as many of the transitional and organizing words and phrases featured in engineered texts for younger students. Reasoning, it seems, is a mediating factor that influences a reader's comprehension.

iStock.com/lisegagne

One of the best ways to promote reasoning is through discussion, especially among students who may be struggling in the development of their reasoning skills.

One of the best ways to promote reasoning is through discussion, especially among students who may be struggling in the development of their reasoning skills. Collaborative reasoning (CR) is an approach to text-based discussion for elementary students designed to encourage students to turn their attention to a broader consideration of the dilemmas posed by a text (Clark et al., 2003). The teacher acts as a facilitator, moderating the discussion and posing deeper questions that require students to use more advanced formal reasoning skills. Traditional recitation discussions can focus students on literal levels of meaning but more rarely move into the deeper kind of text analysis necessary to foster nascent reasoning skills. Figure 3.3 shows a side-by-side comparison of two illustrative discussions. Note that the one on the left, a traditional recitation discussion, features more teacher talk and less sophisticated student responses. In the CR discussion on the right, students talk more and use advanced reasoning skills, and the teacher's input is minimal.

Figure 3.3 Comparing quantity and quality of student response in two types of discussions.

Traditional Recitation Discussion[a]		Collaborative Reasoning Discussion[b]	
T:	Who is the main character of this story?	T:	The big question is, "Should the coach let Ronald play?"
S:	Ronald.	S:	I don't think so, because he couldn't do anything right.
T:	Yes, and what was the problem he faced in this story?	L:	Yeah, if he was on a team he would make people lose.
S:	He couldn't do anything right.	R:	Nobody would want to pick him.
T:	No, what was he trying to do?	J:	I think he should have a chance to be on the team, because then he might have a chance to get better.
S:	He was trying to play baseball.		
T:	Yes, so, our stories usually have a problem and a solution. Remember? We talked about that yesterday. So what was the problem in this story?	B:	That wouldn't be fair, because he would make everybody lose in the meantime.
S:	(no response)	A:	Winning isn't everything.
T:	Okay, B. Can you help S out?	T:	So. What do you think? "Should the coach let Ronald play?"
B:	He wanted to play, but he ran the bases backward and closed his eyes so he couldn't hit the ball.	A:	Maybe the coach could get his dad to practice with him.
T:	Okay, J, what else did he do wrong?	G:	When I first started playing baseball, I was scared I'd get hit by the ball, so I wasn't very good at first, but then after a few practices I got better.
J:	He drew letters in the mud with a stick?		
T:	Why is that a problem?	K:	How would you feel if nobody wanted you to play and called you "Four Eyes" just because you wore glasses? I think they ought to let him play.

(Continued)

Figure 3.3 (Continued)

Traditional Recitation Discussion[a]		Collaborative Reasoning Discussion[b]	
B:	He wasn't paying attention to what his coach was telling him?	B:	But the rest of the team would have to suffer until he got better. Wouldn't that make him feel pretty bad? It would me!
T:	Okay, so the problem in the story was that he couldn't do the things he was supposed to be able to do to play ball, he couldn't hit, he couldn't run, and he didn't pay attention. Is that a problem when you want to play ball?	A:	I think he deserves a chance.
		B:	I disagree, because no one would like him then.
Class:	(in unison) Yeeeeesss.		
T:	So the problem Ronald faced in this story was he kept making mistakes every time he tried to play ball. What happened next?		

Source: Clark, A. M., Anderson, R. C., Kuo, L., Kim, I. H., Archodidou, A., & Nguyen-Jahiel, K. (2003). Collaborative reasoning: Expanding ways for children to talk and think in school, p. 182. *Educational Psychology Review, 15*(2), 181–198. Reproduced with permission of Springer New York LLC in the format Book via Copyright Clearance Center.

[a]Traditional recitation discussion: nine teacher turns, seven student turns (three different students), one whole-class response.

[b]Collaborative reasoning discussion: two teacher turns, twelve student turns (eight different students).

[c]T = teacher; B, S, J, G, K = students

While collaborative reasoning maximizes student talk, this should not be misunderstood to mean that teacher talk is therefore unimportant. There is no evidence that simply having students talk to another in an unguided way will cause critical reasoning to occur (Murphy et al., 2009). Rather, the teacher's role in text-based discussion is crucial to steer discourse into this dimension. The judicious use of prepared questions designed to accomplish this increases the likelihood that critical reasoning instruction will occur. Perhaps the unfortunate habit of letting classroom discussions simply evolve results in too many recitation-style discussions. National Public Radio host Terry Gross, widely lauded as an exceptional interviewer, says that she always knows her "major destination points" and that knowing them is an essential part of her preparation. Likewise, a teacher moderating a text-based discussion should also prepare in advance in order to assure that reasoning is utilized to deepen comprehension.

Reflection: Strategic Awareness

The third dimension of dispositions for learning is reflection on the strategies deployed. You will recall from Block and Lacina's list of

30 reading comprehension strategies in Chapter 2 that many of these were meta-cognitive in nature, such as pausing to reflect, being self-aware of personal perspectives, and engaging in retrospection by looking backward at past events in the story. The ability to reflect upon and think about one's thinking and monitor one's learning are understood to be an essential component of learning (e.g., Flavell, 1979). The term *metacognition* means "above cognition" and works in parallel to the skills and knowledge (cognition) needed to complete complex tasks. And reading for understanding, to be sure, is a complex task. A reader with a high degree of metacognitive awareness approaches reading as a conscious act and recognizes that he is in command of his own understanding. Metacognitive readers don't view the act as simply mowing down line after line of the text. They reflect on their planning and self-evaluate to monitor their comprehension. They notice when they have lost it and manage their strategies to recover meaning. Much like a master craftsperson, these readers not only have a full toolbox; they are able to select the right tool to accomplish the goal.

iStock.com/katleho Seisa

Metacognitive readers don't view the act as simply mowing down line after line of the text. They reflect on their planning and self-evaluate to monitor their comprehension.

More recent reading comprehension research concerns how the brain manages these metacognitive processes, further suggesting that executive function is at play. Executive function (EF) occurs in the prefrontal cortex of the brain and is the controlling mechanism that regulates thinking and goal attainment. As one example, as you read these sentences, your executive functions are ensuring that you are screening out distractions, persisting in reading through the sentences, holding information in working memory, and allowing meaning to continually evolve as you read. Think of these as the "extra-language functions" of reading (Cirino et al., 2019, p. 1820). Your ability to make meaning is not confined to decoding the squiggly black lines on the page, although that is important. The major executive functions of reading are the abilities to shift between mental schemas to make connections among knowledge sets, and continuously update what you know such that you are actively taking in new information and incorporating it into existing schemas.

To be sure, we are educators and not developmental psychologists, much less brain surgeons. However, we are all "brain workers" in the sense that we cultivate learning in our students. As a professional field we understand that learning is not a matter of dumping knowledge into a child's head. The notion of a blank slate went by the wayside about the time that cars began to replace horses as the mode for personal travel. Your understanding of how learning occurs, and the influence of executive function and metacognition, makes it possible to create the conditions that foster reflection and strategic awareness for readers.

One evidence-based approach for fostering metacognitive awareness of reading comprehension strategies is reciprocal teaching (Palincsar & Brown, 1984). Since its development, the effectiveness of the approach has been seen in a wide range of students, whether varied in terms of ability, language proficiency, or reading levels (Galloway, 2003; Rosenshine & Meister, 1994). Reciprocal teaching (RT) is a process for students to enact in small groups to discuss a piece of text. Importantly, a major goal is for students to coconstruct the meaning of the text through dialogic instruction. There are four specific comprehension processes that students enact with intention and reflect upon at specified points in the text:

- *Summarizing* to identify main points and organize them in a coherent way

- *Predicting* both as a means for setting the purpose of reading and to speculate on what information will come next in the reading

- *Questioning* in order to assure accuracy and understanding within the group, especially in posing literal and inferential questions to one another

- *Clarifying* the meaning of unfamiliar words, phrases, and concepts

Thus, readers jointly read and discuss a text that has been segmented into shorter passages. The incremental nature of the stopping points is intended to foster a habit of periodically pausing to reflect on one's understanding. Just as crucial is the dialogue between readers, sometimes in the company of the teacher. Unfortunately, the dialogic element of reciprocal teaching is often lost, with the emphasis placed solely on the four strategies themselves, which the originator of RT termed a "lethal mutation" (Palincsar et al., 2019, p. 158). However, the original research was born out of examinations of effective teacher practices during reciprocal teaching activities, specifically in "requesting that students elaborate on their ideas, (b) restoring direction to the discussion when it began to meander, (c) reworking students' contributions so that they were integrated into the discussion, and (d) modeling the flexible and opportunistic use of the strategies" (Palincsar et al., 2019, p. 158).

Students need guidance in order to develop the strategic awareness needed to comprehend at deeper levels. Simply teaching students about the procedure and then hoping for the best is not sufficient. This guidance comes in two forms:

- The teacher's focus on developing the strategic thinking of the students so that they can increasingly enact reciprocal teaching on their own

- Structures that further promote this kind of higher-order thinking

Ninth-grade English teacher Donnell Washington uses a reciprocal teaching note-taking guide to extend his students' strategic awareness (see Figure 3.4). His class is reading *Between the World and Me* (Coates, 2015), an epistolary written by a Black father to his adolescent son. Mr. Washington selected a passage from the book for his students to examine more closely using RT as a vehicle for building strategic awareness.

"I selected a section of the book that compares the juvenile justice system with the school system, but Coates doesn't make it easy to see the relationship between the two," said Mr. Washington. "I want them to wrestle with this."

Figure 3.4 Reciprocal teaching note-taking guide.

Members:	Learning Intention:
Date:	
Text:	

During Reading	After Reading
Your Predictions:	Were your predictions accurate? Why or why not?
Section 1:	
Section 2:	
Section 3:	
Your Questions:	Do you have unanswered questions?
Section 1:	
Section 2:	
Section 3:	
Your Clarifications:	What tools did you use to clarify your understanding?
Section 1:	
Section 2:	
Section 3:	

Summary Statement of Complete Reading:

Source: Fisher, D., Frey, N., & Hattie, J. (2017). *Teaching literacy in the visible learning classroom, grades 6–12*, p. 120. Corwin. Used with permission.

 Available for download at **resources.corwin.com/comprehension**

The teacher joins small groups throughout the process, listening in and at times facilitating, in order to steer the discourse toward deeper comprehension and to raise their awareness of the strategies they are using. He joins Axel, Marietta, Gael, and Marcus just after they read the following passage:

> I came to see the streets and the schools as arms of the same beast. One enjoyed the official power of the state while the other enjoyed its implicit sanction. But fear and violence were the weaponry of both. Fail in the streets and the crews would catch you slipping and take your body. Fail in the schools and you would be suspended and sent back to those same streets, where they would take your body. And I began to see those two arms in relation—those who failed in the schools justified their destruction in the streets. The society could say, "He should have stayed in school," then washed its hands of him. (Coates, 2015, p. 33)

Mr. Washington listens as the four students work their way through the comprehension strategies. However, he is surprised when their discussion turns to clarification. When Gael asks if anything needs to be clarified, the other three shake their heads no.

"I'm going to challenge that," says the teacher. "What's the metaphor he's using?" Marietta and Marcus both quickly reply, "a two-armed beast," but Mr. Washington asks, "Tell me more about that. What does Coates mean when he says that?"

After a pause, Gael offers, "Well, I think what he's saying is damned if you do, damned if you don't. 'Cuse my language, but that's it."

The teacher chuckles and then says, "Let's go with that. Who can add to that?"

Axel responds, "Yeah, Gael's right. Like Coates is saying that the system is going to get you one way or another, like you're a marked man because you're Black."

Mr. Washington nods, "OK, so who might disagree? Does anyone have another take?"

Now Marcus joins the discussion. "I don't know so much that it's disagreement, but I think there's more to it than just you're gonna fail no matter what. Like he says in this last line, 'The society could say, "He should have stayed in school," then washed its hands of him.' That's cold, man. Not just you're gonna fail 'cause you're Black, but that society is gonna be all happy about it 'cause you proved them right."

Mr. Washington lets the boy's words hang in the air and then says, "That's profound, and you got to the heart of it. And I want you to notice how all four of you got there. You started by saying you didn't need clarification, but look where you got. It's more than just knowing the words. I made you slow down with my questions. But you used your own thinking tools to get there. So, let's think about the tools you used to clarify your understanding. It's right there on the note-taking guide. How'd you get there?"

Marietta responds, "Well, the pausing helped, and another was that Axel added ideas to Gael's," stopping to write these down as she speaks.

"And ya'll gave me some air to disagree and let me figure out what I wanted to say," said Marcus. "Like, searching for the meaning."

The English teacher nods. "Now I'm going to challenge you one more time to another conversation before you move on. Try some retrospection. What's this point have to do with the last passage you read? About the old films of the civil rights workers. Has your understanding of that passage changed now that Coates has discussed the two-handed beast?" Mr. Washington gets up. "I'm going to join another group. Can't wait to hear what you think when we discuss this later as a class."

Relating: Social Sophistication

The last dimension of dispositions for learning has to do with the fundamental nature of humans—we are social animals. We learn through the actions and ideas of others. Even when learning independently, such as when reading, we are interacting with someone else, in this case the author. Our spoken and written communication systems make it possible to share ideas and build knowledge together. This is certainly the case in classrooms, where much of the learning occurs among students in large and small groups, both teacher led and student directed. To be sure, a student with well-developed social skills is perceived as more competent by peers and is therefore more able to benefit from the learning potential of the classroom environment (Mashburn et al., 2009). As well, students with higher vocabulary skills benefit to a higher degree from peer-mediated learning activities, as they possess more sophisticated language skills to express needs, resolve problems, and interact positively with others (Mashburn et al., 2009).

A newer line of research is exploring the relationship among social skills, vocabulary, and reading comprehension (see Figure 3.5). Findings in the last decade suggest a dynamic and reciprocal nature among all three for elementary students. Sparapani and colleagues (2018) examined quantitative and qualitative measures of the three constructs (social skills, vocabulary, and reading comprehension), discovering that growth in one resulted in similar growth in the other two. Conversely, students who did not progress on a pace with classmates in vocabulary, reading comprehension, or social skills similarly failed to make progress in the other two areas. The relationship between reading comprehension and social skills is especially fascinating. The researchers suggest that social skills such as perceiving the perspectives of others affords students a higher degree of understanding of narrative texts. As the authors noted,

> Comprehending narrative text engages social-cognitive skills, challenging readers to empathize with story characters, consider others' perspectives and intentions, make predictions, interpret problems, and generate solutions. . . . To closely read and analyze narrative text might provide a rich platform for social learning in addition to supporting [reading comprehension]. (p. 165)

Notably, the opposite appears to be true, as students with poor reading comprehension skills feel a loss of relatedness to their peers, triggering a downward spiral of withdrawal academically and socially (Trzesniewski et al., 2006). In addition, they are not able to benefit to the same degree in understanding about the social relationships of characters in books, vicariously learning about dilemmas and how they are resolved (Mashburn et al., 2009).

> **Findings in the last decade suggest a dynamic and reciprocal nature among social skills, vocabulary, and reading comprehension.**

Figure 3.5 The reciprocal relationship among social skills, vocabulary, and reading comprehension.

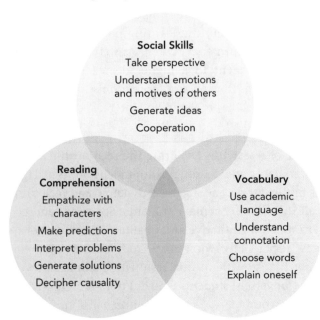

The thing is, dispositions are contagious. Fostering a will for reading comes through the conditions we create in our classrooms for students to witness the dispositions of others. We previously discussed two text-based discussion protocols—collaborative reasoning and reciprocal teaching. Collaborative reasoning provides students with a critical-analytic framework in which to function in order to interrogate arguments and evidence within a text. Reciprocal teaching encourages students to think closely about their strategic approaches to text. But reading dispositions are also about the social sophistication of and interactions among a group of fellow readers. Some texts portray vivid examples of the human condition and demand to be discussed from this angle. In turn, they provide children and adolescents with the chance to engage empathetically with characters, and to learn about cultural and belief systems that are similar to and different from their own.

Grand conversations (GC), an expressive text-based discussion protocol, can provide a forum for just such occasions (Eeds & Wells,

1989). Think of all the times you've seen a film with friends and spilled out of the theater eager to talk with them about what you just saw. No one is in charge of the discussion. Everyone talks about their opinions and wonderings and listens to the others without anyone directing the process. Grand conversations tap into the same kind of energy about texts. The teacher's role is mostly

Researchers suggest that social skills such as perceiving the perspectives of others affords students a higher degree of understanding of narrative texts.

as a member of the group, although setting the stage is essential. These discussions are launched with an essential question designed by the teacher. In addition, language frames can scaffold student discussion to shape ways for students to forward ideas, and to disagree and challenge one another without alienating others (see Figure 3.6 for language frames for text-based discussions).

Figure 3.6 Language frames for text-based discussions.

Paraphrasing the Ideas of Others	Asking for More Information
I think you're saying that . . .	I don't think I understand yet. Could you say more about . . . ?
Is it fair to say that you mean . . . ?	I don't understand why . . .
Am I right that you are saying . . . ?	Can you explain why . . . ?
Agreeing and Adding On	**Disagreeing**
I agree with _____ and I have a similar idea about . . .	I see that situation differently because . . .
_____'s point was important because it helped me . . .	At first, I thought _____ but now I think___ because . . .
When ____ mentioned _____, I started thinking about . . .	From my point of view . . .
	I see it differently because . . .

(Continued)

Figure 3.6 (Continued)

Introducing Ideas	Golden Lines: *Be sure to tell us the page number and paragraph first.*
What do you think of . . . ?	I'd like to read this sentence so we can discuss it . . .
My opinion of _____ is because . . .	I was moved when the author wrote . . .
The author said that _____ and that was interesting to me because . . .	I like how the author said . . .
The character that was most interesting to me is _____ because . . .	

Asking Great Questions of Each Other
Why do you think that is so?
What do you feel is right?
What surprised you about . . . ?
What did you like best?
What did you not like?

Teresa Dominguez's fifth-grade class has finished reading *Fish In a Tree* (Hunt, 2015), a novel about Ally, whose frequent school changes ("seven schools in seven years") have allowed her to mask a dark secret: She can't read. Her latest teacher, however, sees through her disruptive and distracting behavior, and over the course of the book she finds a band of misfits and the strength to confront an undiagnosed disability. Ms. Dominguez has utilized grand conversations for years, noting the importance of being responsive to each class's unique community of learners. This year's class, she has found, seems to profit from having initial small group GC discussions before coming together as a whole class. Therefore, she uses two essential questions. The first one, for discussion in small groups, draws on a quote used in the novel. Ms. Dominguez projects it for the class to see:

> "Everyone is smart in different ways. But if you judge a fish by its ability to climb a tree, it will live its life believing it is stupid." What does this quote mean to Ally, and to you?

The teacher moves from group to group to listen to the conversations. Each table has several copies of language frames in clear protectors to further support their discussion. Many of the students are English learners, and the language frames further scaffold their academic and social language skills. After about 10 minutes, Ms. Dominguez invites the class to arrange their chairs into a circle so they can extend their GC across the class.

"I heard some really interesting ideas in your groups, and I'll bet you did, too. Who would like to get us started about this first essential question?" asks the teacher.

Clarisa raises her hand, and Ms. Dominguez reminds the group that in conversations people talk with one another. Clarisa smiles and then says, "Our group talked about how Ally had one idea of smart, like school smart, and Mr. Daniels [the teacher in the book] and her new friends helped her to see she was other kinds of smart, too."

Paloma nodded, "That's what we talked about, too. But could you or someone else tell us where you thought it changed for her? Like going from thinking she was dumb to knowing she was smart?" For several minutes after, students in the class add ideas, point to passages in the book, and clarify their thinking. Soon Ms. Dominguez is ready to pose the second essential question. Again, she projects it so the entire class can refer back to it:

> Ally talks about being labeled like a soup can. What are the labels the main characters get stuck with? Are there advantages and disadvantages to labels? How do labels affect you?

There is a noticeable shift in the conversation. While students talk initially about labels like "slow reader," "poor," and "nerd" for characters in the book, their discussion soon moves to their own lives. The children of this community are troubled by the rhetoric about immigration and language. Some of them reveal how they or other family members have been the target of hate speech. Julián, whose family traces their history back five generations as ranchers in their county, talks about how his older sister was told to "go back where she came from."

Julián shook his head. "People can see brown skin and hear us speak Spanish, and they think they know everything about us." The conversation is now no longer about the book alone. Ms. Dominguez allows it to evolve as the students offer support for one another.

She then shifts the conversation one more time, asking, "How can we as a classroom community fight against the labels we give to one another?"

Again, the students discuss how labels affect one another, from being called "popular" or "athletic" to "shy" and "hyper." Hugo adds, "It's bullying, really. Like, we say that we'll always be kind to each other, but then we put people in a box and we say, 'That's who you have to be.' Bullying isn't just calling people names."

Sonia immediately adds, "I totally agree, Hugo. Bullying can happen when we label people, because we don't let them become who they can be."

The expressive nature of a GC provides students with a means to link what they are reading to their own social stances. Some of our favorite texts remain so because of the lessons they provide within the safe spaces of the pages of a book.

Not all texts should be discussed using this format. The dialogic activity in the classroom should match the purposes for the reading. Our students' reading comprehension is enhanced and deepened when we pair texts with aligned discussion protocols. A critical-analytic stance is served well through collaborative reasoning, while expressive responses can be elicited through a literature-based protocol such as grand conversations (Murphy et al., 2009). When the purpose for reading is to simultaneously interrogate the information and one's own thinking, reciprocal teaching is a good bet. The urge to talk about what we have read is an undeniable one, but too often that will is crushed by elaborate rituals that squelch the urge to communicate with one another. There are several other structures that allow students to talk with each other about texts, including the following:

> The urge to talk about what we have read is an undeniable one, but too often that will is crushed by elaborate rituals that squelch the urge to communicate.

- *Socratic seminars*. Some texts demand longer discussions: "An ambiguous and appealing short story, a pair of contrasting primary documents in social studies, or an article on a controversial approach to an ongoing scientific problem" (Filkins, 2012, ¶ 4). Socratic seminars can be a type of judgment task, especially when students are asked to speculate and make predictions. Students sit in a circle so they can face one another, text in hand. The teacher serves as the facilitator of the discussion, posing open-ended questions to the group. If the conversation begins to veer off track, the teacher can restate the open-ended question. This can be a challenge for students, who are conditioned to direct their comments to the teacher, not to one another. As the facilitator, the teacher should resist the urge to interject more than is necessary, or to offer evaluative statements. The Paideia Society advises that closing questions focus on the students' personal experiences and insights, so that they can make connections to their own lives.

- *Text rendering experience.* Eighth-grade social studies teacher Ray Wilkins uses a process called text rendering experience (TRE) to locate the essence of a document (Baron, 2007; see Figure 3.7). "I have them use TRE when the document is dense, but the reading is fairly short," he said. Students read the document independently, and then review it a second time to mark their most meaningful sentence, phrase, and word. "There's no right answer," Mr. Wilkins reminds them. "Go with your gut." Students read the contents of the Bill of Rights in the U.S. Constitution first to get a sense of the overall document, and then a second time to note their three choices. In groups of five, the students worked through the three rounds of the protocol (see sidebar for details). Lexus's group identified the following phrases and words:

  o enjoy the right
  o right of the people
  o security of a free State
  o life or limb
  o freedom of speech
  o consent
  o peaceably
  o jeopardy
  o respecting
  o free

"The first thing I see is how much our list is about rights and freedoms," she said. "I guess that makes sense, 'cause it's the Bill of Rights and all." Oliver added, "But I think we also picked words that aren't about people fighting, like *peaceably* and *respecting*." For the next few minutes, the group discussed the intersection of rights and conflict, noting that "enjoying the right" was key. Mr. Wilkins then gathered all the groups together to continue the discussion. "You've had a chance to get some first impressions of the Bill of Rights," he said. "Now let's dive into them so we've got a better sense of what each means and what it means for society."

- *Jigsaw* (Aronson et al., 1978) is useful for longer and more complex documents. Jigsaw is a three-step process in which students are members of two groups, an expert group and a home group. The text is divided, and members of the same expert group have the same part of the text. Students meet in their expert groups to discuss the text. They then move to their home group in which members have different sections of the text, and they provide information to their peers about the content that they read. Finally, students return to their expert groups to talk about how their part of the text fit into the whole text. This strategy provides students multiple opportunities to talk about the text.

Figure 3.7 Text rendering experience protocol.

1. Students read the text all the way through, and then read it a second time to select a powerful sentence, phrase, and word. Each should come from a different part of the document.

2. Students work in collaborative groups and select a facilitator and a scribe. The facilitator manages the process, while the scribe records the phrases and words identified. (Sentences are not recorded.)

3. *Round 1*: Each member reads his or her selected *sentence* with no further commentary by the individual or the group.

4. *Round 2*: Each member reads his or her selected *phrase* with no further commentary by the individual or the group. The scribe lists the phrases so that the group can see them.

5. *Round 3*: Each member reads his or her selected *word* with no further commentary by the individual or the group. The scribe lists the words so that the group can see them.

6. The members of the group discuss their impressions of the document based on the sentences, phrases, and words that were stated.

7. The members of the group discuss new understandings of the document that have emerged.

There are many other instructional approaches that encourage discussion and dialogue about texts. There are times, of course, when instruction should be tightly controlled, as when introducing new skills. But fostering the will of reading comprehension requires opportunities for students to expand their thinking in the company of peers and under the watchful eye of a teacher. It's knowing what to be tight on and what to be loose on. The best tools you have at your disposal for fostering the dispositions to read—resilience, resourcefulness, reflection, and relating—are the students themselves.

Fostering the will of reading comprehension requires opportunities for students to expand their thinking in the company of peers and under the watchful eye of a teacher.

Creating the Classroom Conditions for Will to Flourish

Reading comprehension instruction focused on will begins with an invitation to engage and interact with text more freely across more volumes of text. But like any invitation, it must be given within a climate that is conducive to fostering motivation and engagement. The social context can promote or inhibit learning, regardless of an individual's motivation. A harsh and punitive environment shuts down the learning. In contrast, one that is psychologically safe, physically comfortable, culturally sustaining, and designed with the learners' needs in mind can expand possibilities. Learning is accelerated when the student can answer the three questions that drive all of us (Fisher et al., 2016, p. 27):

1. What am I learning?

2. Why am I learning it?

3. How will I know I have learned it?

These questions speak to the vital nature of choice and relevance in learning. When students are able to exercise choice, and are exposed to topics and materials that are relevant to their lives, the will to read increases. They are no longer reading for someone else; they are doing it for themselves.

We're not pie-in-the-sky dreamers when it comes to the motivation to read. All three of us have been classroom teachers and school administrators for our entire professional careers. We have all witnessed and experienced the Wednesday afternoon rainy day doldrums, when it has been cold and gray for days, it's February, and the collective energy level of the adult and the students in the room are at the lowest point of the year. In fact, it is just that kind of day when the structures you have created to ensure choice and relevance happen will save you. They can be the spark you and your students need.

Teaching Practices to Build Choice in Your Classroom

Two of us are English teachers, and we would like to leave the practice of assigning a single, whole-class novel per quarter for at-home reading in the last century. Nothing is more dreadful than dragging 35 listless adolescents through a book they have little interest in. Before you think that we are dismissing the importance of reading contemporary and historical literary and informational texts, please hear us out. We agree that all students should interact with an array of readings before they graduate from high school. But they also need to exercise some choice in what we read together as a class and what they read individually.

Our units of study are organized around an essential question that is designed to be thought provoking and not easily answered. Our targeted book for whole-class instruction (in the classroom) extends from that essential question, and it is a complex reading designed to stretch students' skills and knowledge. As teachers, we share several potential targeted books aligned to the essential question, and students share their opinions about what they might like to read as a class. We also offer a range of related readings for them to select from to read independently or collaboratively. These texts cover a quantitatively and qualitatively wide range of readers. We place special attention on choosing independent readings that represent a diversity of author voices in terms of gender, culture, time period, and perspective (see Figure 3.8 for one unit of study).

> We would like to leave the practice of assigning a single, whole-class novel per quarter for at-home reading in the last century.

Figure 3.8 Book list for "Does Gender Matter?" unit of study.

High-Interest Books You Can Easily Read

A Single Shard (Linda Sue Park, 2011)

Brian's Winter (Gary Paulsen, 1995)

It Ain't So Awful, Falafel (Firoozeh Dumas, 2017)

Riding Freedom (Pam Munoz Ryan, 1999)

The Breadwinner Trilogy (Deborah Ellis, 2008)

Coraline (graphic novel and prose novel; Neil Gaiman, 2002)

The Graveyard Book (Neil Gaiman, 2009)

Wringer (Jerry Spinelli, 2004)

Young Adult Books That Might Challenge Your Reading and Thinking Skills

Breathing Underwater (Alex Finn, 2002)

Give a Boy a Gun (Todd Strasser, 2002)

House of Purple Cedar (Tim Tingle, 2014)

I Am Not Your Perfect Mexican Daughter (Erika Sanchez, 2018)

Inside Out and Back Again (Thanhha Lai, 2013)

Leviathan (Scott Westerfield, 2010)

Luna (Julie Anne Peters, 2006)

Mexican White Boy (Matt de la Pena, 2008)

Persopolis (graphic novel; Marjane Satrapi, 2004)

Seen the Glory: A Novel of the Battle of Gettysburg (John Hough, Jr., 2010)

The Chocolate War (Robert Cormier, 1974)

The Color Purple (Alice Walker, 1982)

The Poet X (Acevedo, 2017)

The Yellow Wallpaper (short story; Charlotte Perkins Gilman, 1892)

To Kill a Mockingbird (Harper Lee, 1960)

Complex But Interesting Texts That Require Thought and Effort

A Doll's House (play; Henrik Ibsen, 1879)

Americanah (Chimamanda Ngozi Adichie, 2014)

Brokeback Mountain (short story; Annie Proulx, 1997)

Death of a Salesman (play; Arthur Miller, 1949)

How the Garcia Girls Lost Their Accents (Julia Alvarez, 1991)

How We Became Human (poetry; Joy Harjo, 2004)

Middlesex (Jeffrey Eugenides, 2002)

Norwegian Wood (Haruki Murakami, 2000)

Pride and Prejudice (Jane Austen, 1813)

The Handmaid's Tale (Margaret Atwood, 1985)

The Namesake (Jhumpa Lahiri, 2004)

The Woman Warrior (Maxine Hong Kingston, 1989)

Things Fall Apart (Chinua Achebe, 1958)

Twelfth Night (play; William Shakespeare)

White Teeth (Zadie Smith, 2001)

Wuthering Heights (Emily Bronte, 1850)

One unit was organized under the essential question, "Does gender matter?" and the target book for the entire class was *Lord of the Flies* (Golding, 1954). In addition, students chose at least one text to read on their own. Books are organized in categories so that students can make decisions about their investment in time:

- High-Interest Books You Can Easily Read

- Young Adult Books That Might Challenge Your Reading and Thinking Skills

- Complex But Interesting Texts That Require Thought and Effort

Students write literacy letters every week as a way to journal directly with the teacher (Frey et al., 2009). They use the format of a friendly letter ("Dear Mr. Fisher") and follow a prescribed organizational plan for the content. The first paragraph contains the name of the book and author as well as an update on what is happening in the book to this point. The second paragraph addresses the specific prompt for the week as it relates to the essential question and the whole-class target book. For instance, one week during the unit, we asked for them to write speculatively about how societal expectations of gender were impacting the antagonist and protagonist in their selected text. The third paragraph is a short one, as they rate their reading experience thus far.

The first week's literacy letter prompt is a generic one, as students have only just begun to read their choice book:

> In your letter this week, write about the book's genre and any connections you may have with the book. Can you connect and identify with the characters? Does this book remind you of any other book you have read? Does this book make you think of anything that is happening in the world? This prompt can be answered no matter what the genre is! Don't forget to rate your book 1–10!

The choice selection and the literacy letters accomplish two important goals. The first is that we want our students to engage in comparative literature as a natural extension of what readers do. With each text read, we build a mental library we use to evaluate what we are currently reading. We are all, as young-adult book author Jason Reynolds says, "databases in motion." We want to ignite connections to build bonds with books. The second goal relates to the literacy letters themselves. This is a form of dialogic journal that provides us with a means to engage in discussion about the text in more personal ways. Knowing that Ishran is reading *The Namesake* (Lahiri, 2004) gives us a topic to talk about with him when he arrives in class, and a reason to connect him to a few other students in different class periods who are reading the same book. The invitational nature of reading as a means to interact about a shared experience appeals to the emotional strength and relatedness that compose positive learning dispositions.

Building classroom choice

Choice is not limited to adolescents. When Nancy taught in the primary grades, students voted each day on the interactive read-aloud text they would hear after lunch. When Doug taught in fifth grade, his teaching team previewed books for literature circles so that students could choose their top three, and then the team organized the books based on the students' preferences (not reading levels). This is not an exhaustive list of possibilities, but rather a reminder that reading choice can be infused into classrooms when there is a teacher willing to make it a priority.

Teaching Practices to Build Relevance in Your Classroom

Reading is about making meaning, but what about making reading *meaningful*? Reading becomes meaningful when it is seen as relevant by the reader. It is more than just interest (although that is a factor). Readings are relevant when they address issues of identity, perspective, and experience in ways that resonate on a personal level. What resonates is dynamic and can't be easily determined simply by sizing up the demographics of a class or ordering a few extra titles by writers of color. How else could we explain these titles, all of which students requested in a single week at our school?

- *Make Your Bed: Little Things That Can Change Your Life and Maybe the World* (McRaven, 2018)

- *Lowriders in Space* (Camper & Raul the Third, 2014)

- *Aesop's Fables*

- *Manga in Theory and Practice: The Craft of Creating* Manga (Hirohiko, 2017)

- *Guinness World Records 2019*

- *The Price of Independence: The Economics of Early Adulthood* (Danzinger, 2008)

- *Ace of Cakes: Inside the World of Charm City Cakes* (Goldman, 2009)

- *Her* (Jeanty, 2017)

- *College and Career Success* (Fralick, 2017)

- *Siddhartha* (Hesse, 1998)

If you think you have a mental picture of who the students might be, you would probably be surprised. *Lowriders in Space* was requested by a Muslim girl in 9th grade who wears a hijab. *Siddhartha* was requested by a Latino English learner in 11th grade who is making strides in his reading but isn't yet at grade level. *Ace of Cakes* was requested by an African American 10th grader who shines on the basketball court. You just never know what will appeal to a reader.

That said, there is much that is known about locating books that are relevant to students. Bishop's 1990 seminal essay "Mirrors, Windows, and Sliding Glass Doors" spurred a generation of educators to stock classrooms and curricula with literary and informational texts that are culturally sustaining and that invite students into new worlds:

Readings are relevant when they address issues of identity, perspective, and experience in ways that resonate on a personal level.

iStock.com/fstop123

Books are sometimes windows, offering views of worlds that may be real or imagined, familiar or strange. These windows are also sliding glass doors, and readers have only to walk through in imagination to become part of whatever world has been created and recreated by the author. When lighting conditions are just right, however, a window can also be a mirror. Literature transforms human experience and reflects it back to us, and in that reflection we can see our own lives and experiences as part of the larger human experience. Reading, then, becomes a means of self-affirmation, and readers often seek their mirrors in books. (p. ix)

There are nuances within Bishop's advice that may be overlooked. The importance of children and adolescents seeing themselves in the books they read is crucial, and selecting books featuring protagonists similar to our students and topics familiar to them is wise. But we also need to be able to create what Bishop calls "the lighting conditions" such that other texts are presented in new ways that resonate with students. We used *Lord of the Flies* as a vehicle for discussing gender issues in order to tilt the window of shipwrecked midcentury British school boys such that students might see themselves in societal expectations of gendered roles. Textual relevance, therefore, can be "*empathetic*, or mirror-like, connections, or *sympathetic*, or window-like, connections" (Sciurba, 2017, p. 372).

The need for culturally sustaining literary and informational texts cannot be overstated. Despite Bishop's call—now 40 years old—for books that feature the stories of the lives of the children that fill our schools, relatively few texts (23%) published in 2018 were by or about people of color. Compare that to the fact that 27% of published titles were about animals or inanimate objects such as trucks or water (Cooperative Children's Book Center, n.d.). Award-winning books identified by organizations dedicated to highlighting quality children's and adolescents' literary and informational texts are an excellent place to begin updating classroom and school libraries and the curriculum materials used by teachers. A short list of lists can be found in Figure 3.9.

Identifying relevant texts is a hit-or-miss proposition if you don't know your students well. Find out about your students' interests,

Figure 3.9 Book awards lists for locating quality literature.

Book Award	Focus
Schneider Family Book Award (ala.org/awardsgrants/schneider-family-book-award)	Honors an author or illustrator for a book that embodies an artistic expression of the disability experience for child and adolescent audiences
Coretta Scott King Book Award (ala.org/rt/emiert/cskbookawards)	Honors outstanding African American authors and illustrators of books for children and young adults that demonstrate an appreciation of African American culture and universal human values
Pura Belpré Award (ala.org/alsc/awardsgrants/bookmedia/belpremedal)	Honors a Latinx writer and illustrator whose work best portrays, affirms, and celebrates the Latinx cultural experience in an outstanding work of literature for children and youth
Asian/Pacific American Award (apalaweb.org/awards/literature-awards/)	Honors and recognizes individual work about Asian/Pacific Islander Americans and their heritage, based on literary and artistic merit
Award for Excellence in Nonfiction for Young Adults (ala.org/yalsa/)	Honors the best nonfiction book published for young adults (ages 12–18)
Indigenous Voices Award (indigenousliterarystudies.org/-indigenous-voices-award)	Supports Indigenous literary production in its diversity and complexity, honoring the sovereignty of Indigenous creative voices while rejecting cultural appropriation
High Plains Book Awards (highplainsbookawards.org/nominations-and-criteria/)	Recognizes authors and/or literary works that examine and reflect life on the High Plains of North America
American Indian Youth Literature Award (ailanet.org/activities/american-indian-youth-literature-award/)	Honors writing and illustrations by and about Native Americans and Indigenous peoples of North America that present Indigenous North American peoples in the fullness of their humanity
The National Book Awards for Fiction, Nonfiction, Poetry, Translated Literature, and Young People's Literature (www.nationalbook.org/)	Celebrates the "best literature in America" (NBA website)

Source: Fisher, D., Frey, N., & Savitz, R.S. (2020). *Teaching hope and resilience for students experiencing trauma: Creating safe and nurturing classrooms for learning*, pp. 72–73. Teachers College Press.

their reading lives, and their opinions about the books they want to read. Kendall Nielsen, a second-grade teacher in a semirural community that has welcomed refugees from around the world, conducts reader interviews with her students to make decisions about the texts she selects. "I grew up in this town, and I didn't get much exposure to people from different places. But I also didn't get to learn about them in the books I read in school, either" she said. "That's been a real loss for me, and I want to make sure that doesn't happen to my students."

Ms. Nielsen uses a reader interview to learn more about each of her students (Sharma & Christ, 2017). In addition to learning a bit about their past educational experiences and family celebrations, she uses books from the classroom to find out about their perceptions of reading. The teacher selects about eight books that represent a range of genres and text complexity. Some are books that she believes might be of interest and that perhaps the student has already read. In addition, she selects a few that might not be so obvious. "It's definitely a bit of roaming around with the student, in terms of having a good sample," she said. "Sometimes I end up grabbing some different books midinterview, because the ones I have are not working for the student." A copy of the reader interview can be found in Figure 3.10.

When she interviewed Hani, she learned that the girl had emigrated from Somalia with her family three years ago and had attended the school since kindergarten. Ms. Nielsen learned about Hani's favorite part of Eid al-Fitr ("cambaabur!" she exclaimed, referring to the sweet bread sprinkled with sugar and spices that her mother makes). The teacher then directed Hani's attention to the array of books on the table in front of them. When Ms. Nielsen asked Hani to choose a book and explain why it was a good fit, Hani chose the book *Planets* (Carney, 2012). As she paged through the book, Hani talked about the photographs and illustrations. "I want to be an astronaut who takes pictures in space," she said, "and then I want to make books about space for other kids to read." When asked about books that took place in a place she had been before, she chose *The Nose Tree* (Hutton, 1981). "I'm not positive but I think it might be in Germany," she said, referring to the fairy tale. "I don't remember Germany 'cause I was too little. But my family talks about being there before we came to America."

Figure 3.10 Reader interview.

Demographic Information	What is your name?
	How old are you?
	How long have you attended this school?
	Where did you attend school before this?
Family members and living arrangements	Tell me about your family.
	Do you have any pets? What do you like best about where you live?
Favorite family activities	What are some activities that you do weekly with your family?
	What kinds of celebrations or holidays do you and your family enjoy?
Perceptions about reading	Do you like to read? Why or why not?
	Do you read at home? How often?
	Do you prefer to read with someone else or by yourself? Do you think it's important to know how to read? Why or why not?
Perceptions of reading: Book display	Do you see anything here that you would like to read? Why or why not?
	What book do you think would be:
	a) Just-right for you to read. What makes it just-right?
	b) Too easy for you to read. What makes it too easy?
	c) Too hard for you to read. What makes it too hard?
Perceptions about cultural relevance of texts	Which of these books do you think has characters that are like you? How are they like you?
	Which of these books takes place in places that you've been before? How are they like places you've been?
	Which of these books has characters that talk like you? Which of these books has an event that is like an experience that you had?
	What was your experience and how does it relate to the book?

Source: Sharma, S. A., & Christ, T. (2017). Five steps toward successful culturally relevant text selection and integration, p. 297. *Reading Teacher, 71*(3), 295–307.

After she finished interviewing Hani, Ms. Nielsen made some notes herself. "I learned a lot about her, and I realized that I need to update my space collection. But I've also got some new ideas about what she might like."

Conclusion

A student's will to read is an important lever we can utilize to promote reading comprehension. As important as the skills of reading are, they alone will not sufficiently build the mental attitude, habits, and inclinations to read without cajoling. And a child with a disposition toward reading has a world of possibilities—what Bishop (1990) called the sliding glass doors they can step through to a new experience.

As teachers, there is much we can do to create an emotional climate in the classroom that strengthens the will of reading. The first is to cultivate an atmosphere of inquiry that encourages students to find out about the social, physical, and biological world around them. Bringing interesting print, digital, and multimedia texts into the classroom is easier than it has ever been. Once these texts are located, it is up to teachers to use them to invite students into the reading world, as Ms. Harrison did with Nyah at the beginning of this chapter. In addition, we need to sensitively interrupt feelings of anxiety and inferiority around reading that can creep in when students are faced with challenging texts. There is a special cruelty in standing in the way of a child who wants to read a book. The colored dots on the spines of books that limit choices to current reading "levels" have tyrannized classrooms for too long. Having said that, we must also support students during the challenges experienced while reading complex texts. This is a direct investment in their dispositions, especially in building the characteristics of resilience, resourcefulness, reflection, and relatedness that fuel them.

> There is a special cruelty in standing in the way of a child who wants to read a book. The colored dots on the spines of books that limit choices to current reading "levels" have tyrannized classrooms for too long.

Teaching practices that strengthen the will of reading include an emphasis on choice and relevance to bring print to life. This requires knowing students well in order to better identify texts that are relevant to them (not just the teacher or the curriculum committee). Importantly, relevance includes affirming cultural connections and identities, and encouraging students to read to learn about topics that are meaningful to them. In doing so, we are able to provide more choice and more variety for deeper engagement and motivation to read.

Even when no one is looking.

Thrill in Reading Comprehension

Tre, a fourth-grade student who was becoming more interested in reading, was halfway through *The Janitor's Boy* (Clements, 2001), the story of Jack, a boy who is ashamed when his friends discover that his father is the school janitor. Jack learns that his father has the keys for the entire school and gives in to pressure from his friends to steal them.

"It's sad that he treats his dad like that," Tre said, "like he's embarrassed. But I see why he's thinking about those keys. Man, it'd be cool to get into school at night."

His teacher, Trevor Hill, asked him what he thought Jack would do.

"I dunno. His pops might lose his job. I think it'll all work out, 'cause a story's 'sposed to have a happy ending."

Mr. Hill saw Tre's reference to the ending of story as an opportunity to engage him in critical literacy, so he asked Tre if stories *should* have happy endings. In posing this question, Mr. Hill wanted to nudge Tre to question a commonplace element in stories.

Tre answered quickly. "No. Life's not like that. I like it when everything isn't happy, like in Lemony Snicket [books]. I want to read all of those. There's 13 of them and they all have 13 chapters. I read five so far. So that's 65 chapters I read."

Tre's growth as a reader is captured in that conversation, as the boy elegantly used the reading comprehension skills of summarizing, analyzing, and predicting to discriminate between what stories often do and what he thought they should do. In addition, he voiced his will to read, expressing his preference for a different kind of book. These two elements represent a move from *skill* (strategy) to *will* (disposition). His comments also indicated his growth as a critical reader. That's where the thrill of reading lies. While acknowledging the traditional storytelling form of the happy ending, he also challenged the norms of children's literature. Of course, his connection to the Lemony Snicket series is informative about his development as a reader. Tre is demonstrating a taste for books that are a little edgy, but he still needs the happy endings embedded in the "series of unfortunate events"—after all, those unfortunate Baudelaire children keep escaping Count Olaf's clutches, don't they?

> **Reading should not be a passive consumer experience but rather an active producer one.**

The thrill of comprehension comes when readers get to act upon their private and public worlds. Reading should not be a passive consumer experience but rather an active producer one. It begins with taking a critical stance, as readers learn they can and should ask questions of the text and its context. In addition, we want students to set goals for themselves. Those goals are driven by a need they have to answer questions about themselves and the world, not just to complete a goal sheet given to them by the teacher. We want students to ask and be able to answer the question "What does this text inspire me to do?" We believe that the whole point of comprehension is to take action. To make the world just a little bit better.

Thrill in Reading Comprehension

Reading for deep meaning is at once a process of gathering information and challenging the very same. To leave students with the dangerous assumption that whatever is in print should be accepted at face value puts them at great peril. The notion of bidirectional reading, or what Janks (2019) calls "reading with and against texts" (p. 561), is crucial if students are to critique and not just consume. After all, what is reading ultimately in service of if it fails to build one's identity, wisdom, and empathy for others? What is reading for if it doesn't make a positive impact on readers and their communities? The last lines of David Pearson's speech, shared in Chapter 1, ring in our ears:

Comprehension, which may be important

   If it is on the pathway to . . .

Critical reasoning and problem solving, which may be important

   if it is the pathway to . . .

Action in the world. Changing something that matters.

Art Costa, who developed the habits of mind framework, reminds us that school is not about preparing students for a life of tests, but for the tests of life. The texts students read apprentice them into these life tests in ways that are safe. They can experience the loss of a loved one, the taste of victory when an obstacle is overcome, the shame of letting oneself down and what it takes to get back up again, all through the pages of a book. Harry Potter, Starr Carter, Charlotte the spider, the Mirabel sisters, and the Joad brothers are all imagined figures that have taught us how we might be better versions of ourselves. Stories about Dwight Eisenhower, Sonia Sotomayor, Rumi, Murasaki Shikibu, and Chief Joseph show us how real people did the same.

Cultivating *thrill* in reading comprehension

The thrill of reading comprehension begins with the realization that one possesses power over the text. One's sense of agency—the ability to take action—can be in the small moments of recognizing that one has power over a text even before she can read. Nancy was visiting a kindergarten classroom and sat down next to Beto, who was reading *How the Grinch Stole Christmas!* (Dr. Seuss, 1957). Nancy asked him about the story, and Beto excitedly turned the pages, telling the story in his own free-form way. Then he abruptly stopped, looked at Nancy and said, "I *think* you can read. Can you read it to me?" (In Beto's defense, he had just met Nancy, who had not yet demonstrated any reading skills.) Beto is learning that he can seek resources to accomplish his goal.

Power over texts can come in the form of pursuing one's own inquiry. Sixth grader Ciara wanted to learn more about sickle cell anemia after reading the first chapter of *Look Both Ways: A Tale Told in Ten Blocks* (Reynolds, 2019). "I didn't know it would come up again in the last chapter," she said. "It was a problem I didn't know anything about, and now I want to learn more about it," she said. She has been avidly following the story of Jennelle Stephenson, the first person to receive an experimental gene replacement therapy. "So now I am reading more about gene therapy and what scientists are trying to do," she said. Ciara is learning that a text can be a springboard to new knowledge pathways.

Activism and protest can be sparked by texts. In September 2019, hundreds of thousands of young people from 150 countries marched on Climate Strike Friday as a call to action. Science teachers around the world not only used texts in their classrooms to dispense knowledge about current conditions and future prognostications, but also collaborated with other colleagues and community members to make it possible for students to organize and lead local efforts. Todd and Carly, 11th-grade students at a high school on a Native American reservation, worked with school and tribal leaders to organize a bus trip to transport classmates to the state capitol building. "The statistics are frightening, and it's up to us to change this path we're on," said Carly. "We're doomed as a species if we don't," added Todd. Their reading coupled with their engagement with the world led them to take action about something they feel passionate about.

Reading comprehension requires that students read both *with* and *against* the text.

The thrill of reading comprehension requires three conditions:

- First, the student reads critically, both with and against the text.

- The second is that there is some goal setting—a determination—to accomplish something.

- And the third condition allows for students to take action on the goal.

We are intrigued with the notion of "agitation literacies" as a means for "engagements with texts [that] lead youths to do, think, and be different."
—Muhammad

These three conditions work together to inspire the passion that readers need to achieve in school and in life. In the sections that follow, we will talk about each. The thrill that comes from knowing one's own power is evidenced in small actions and ones on a global scale. We are intrigued with the notion of "agitation literacies" as a means for "engagements with texts [that] lead youths to do, think, and be different" (Muhammad, 2019, p. 352). This piece lists four questions teachers are challenged to ask themselves as they design lessons and map onto the collective skill, will, and thrill of reading comprehension (see Figure 4.1).

The Right and the Responsibility of Criticism

Being critical is healthy. In the United States, being critical is a cornerstone of our democratic government. As citizens we are allowed to assemble and to share our criticisms without fear of reproach. We are encouraged to notice things that need changing. As Winston Churchill noted, "Criticism may not be agreeable, but it is necessary. It fulfils the same function as pain in the human body. It calls attention to an unhealthy state of things." And he was right. Criticism creates change. It's about noticing things that could be better and taking action to improve the situation.

But being critical does not mean being mean. Students need help understanding this distinction. Healthy criticism is constructive and focuses on change and improvement. As Abraham Lincoln wisely suggested, "He has a right to criticize, who has a heart to help." Lincoln's words are worth paying attention to—if we're going to teach students to be critical readers, we must teach them how learn from the gaps or flaws they might see in a text to envision and create something better. Being critical is not an end in itself, but rather the catalyst for taking action. Therein lies the thrill.

> Being critical is not an end in itself, but rather the catalyst for taking action. Therein lies the thrill.

Figure 4.1 Questions for teaching an equity model of literacy learning.

	Reflective Questions for Teachers
Skill	How will my instruction and text selection build students' literacy skills and standards?
Intellect	How will my instruction and text selection build students' knowledge and mental powers?
Identity	How will my instruction and text selection help students learn something about themselves and about others?
Criticality	How will my instruction and text selection engage students' thinking about power, equity, and the disruption of oppression?

Source: Muhammad, G. (2019). Protest, power, and possibilities: The need for agitation literacies, p. 353. *Journal of Adolescent & Adult Literacy, 63*(3), 351–355.

Critical literacy

Fostering Deep Comprehension With Critique

Critical literacy has gained wide acknowledgment in the role it plays in reading comprehension. Critical literacy "views readers as active participants in the reading process and invites them to move beyond passively accepting the text's message to question, examine, or dispute the power relations that exist between readers and authors" (McLaughlin & DeVoogd, 2004, p. 14). The goal of critical literacy is not to criticize a text, but rather to ask important questions about the author, the characters, the information, and the message. The assumption here is that meaning is jointly constructed by the reader and the text, as opposed to the more passive act of extracting the "right" meaning from the text.

People sometimes confuse the habits of critical literacy and critical thinking. Some teachers have said, "Oh, critical literacy, I do that. It's those inferential and interpretative questions in my textbook." Critical literacy does involve critical thinking skills, especially reasoning. As noted in previous chapters, the deductive and inductive reasoning used assists the reader in making meaning, drawing inferences, and analyzing the text structure. However, in critical literacy you don't just dig below the surface to see what makes a text work; you also ask "Is this text working?" and "How is it working?" Students analyze texts closely for issues of unequal power, author's intent, and alternative perspectives. The overarching goal, therefore, is to foster astute, sophisticated readers who will query texts for bias of information and omission of other viewpoints. In a digital age, when sometimes questionable information has a means of being instantly disseminated and consumed, it is essential for students to be able to read critically, lest they be subjected to misinformation. Perhaps this is why a critical literacy approach is increasingly associated with information and communication technology in schools.

> The overarching goal, is to foster astute, sophisticated readers who will query texts for bias of information and omission of other viewpoints.

This is not to say that all texts are filled with misinformation, or that all authors have an ulterior or sinister motive. Rather, it is a recognition that no text is neutral, and in fact never can be. All writing is influenced by the author's viewpoints, style, knowledge, and purpose. When we ask students to "examine the author's craft" or "identify the viewpoint assumed by the author," we are inviting a conversation that bumps up against the edges of critical literacy. These questions prompt our students to think of the authors behind the text. We extend the conversation by encouraging readers to examine the roles of power and class, gender and race, and differing perspectives, in order to raise vital questions of equity. The chart in Figure 4.2 provides examples of how reasoning questions can be transformed into critical literacy questions.

Figure 4.2 Contrasting critical thinking and critical literacy.

Critical *Reasoning* Question	Critical *Literacy* Question
Why did Rosa Park refuse to move?	Why was Rosa Parks's act of defiance empowering to her and others? (power)
The family in this book held a big party for their son. How did the son feel about all these presents?	The family in this book held a big party for their son, with lots of presents. Do you think there are other ways a family can celebrate and show their love? (class)
What's similar between a superhero and a president?	Do superheroes do their own laundry? (gender)
What personal connections did you make to this story?	Do you see yourself represented in this story? (race and identity)
How would you compare the Wicked Witch to Hansel and Gretel?	What story would the Wicked Witch tell about the Hansel and Gretel? (alternative perspectives)

Fostering critical literacy analysis occurs primarily through conversation, when the teacher and students can focus carefully on deep understanding. Consider this conversation between Doug and fourth grader Nayeli about Charlotte, the main character in *Riding Freedom* (Ryan, 1999), the fictionalized account of a girl who disguised herself as a boy in order to make a living as a stagecoach driver in the California gold fields.

Doug: What words would you use to describe Charlie [Charlotte]?

Nayeli: Well, smart, and nice . . . I would say courageous.

Doug: Why courageous?

Nayeli: She did dangerous things . . . like when the bridge collapsed and they fell into the river. But then she worried that the doctor would find out her secret.

Doug: What do you think about that?

Nayeli: I guess I don't know why she didn't just tell people. She was a grown-up; so she didn't have to be a man anymore.

Doug: Why might she want to stay dressed as a man?

Nayeli: Maybe she got used to being a man. Like, she sort of liked the clothes and everyone calling her Charlie.

Doug: Is that OK?

Nayeli: Yeah . . . it's OK. I think her day was easier . . . to be a man. She could go anywhere she wanted.

Doug: Would you want the book to end differently? What if she went back to being Charlotte? Would it be a better ending?

Nayeli: No, I don't think she would be happy. Everyone doesn't have to get married at the end of the story, you know!

In this conversation, Nayeli weighed her perceptions of gender roles against a character who defied the conventions of society. Doug's questions moved from character analysis ("What words would you use to describe Charlie?") to consideration of gender roles and alternative endings of the text. They didn't sit down to have a critical literacy conversation—it was an outgrowth of dialogue between an astute reader and a teacher who encourages students to move beyond the "right answer."

Reading Through a Critical Literacy Lens

For critical literacy to become a disposition, it needs to be integrated into the discourse of the classroom.

In order for critical literacy to become a disposition, it needs to be integrated into the discourse of the classroom. It can't be left to occur only during a unit of critical literacy. In critical literacy classrooms, students are routinely asked to evaluate what they are reading, in their journals and during conferring. They are encouraged to question traditional roles and messages, and their teachers model alternative perspectives for them. Children and adolescents are a simple keystroke away from both information and misinformation. To us, the habit of engaging in a critically literate reading is essential. We focus on three elements of critical literacy in classrooms:

- Question the Commonplace in a Text

- Consider the Role of the Author

- Seek Alternative Perspectives

Question the Commonplace in a Text

One of the many wonderful things about spending time in the company of children is witnessing their ability to cast a new light on the ordinary. Most of us have had the experience of examining an object we have taken for granted—a leaf, let's say—only to have a child ask a startling question we had never before considered. "Does a leaf feel?" sounds profound coming from a person who isn't old enough to cross the street by herself. The same can be said for the ordinary truths accepted in literary and informational texts. Familiar assumptions about the world and its people can retreat from the conscious eye of the reader, like the singular astonishment of a leaf that has long since become part of the background. A critical literacy lens requires that readers seek to disrupt the commonplace through active questioning about topics related to gender, power, class, and race.

iStock.com/Courtney Hale

A critical literacy lens requires that readers seek to disrupt the commonplace through active questioning about topics related to gender, power, class, and race.

One technique to introduce reading with this critical lens is to challenge students to examine the role of heroes and villains in stories. Many readers are eager to cast the stories they read as good versus evil, with unflawed champions battling unrepentant scoundrels. Part of this is developmental—a child's world is fairly well demarcated—but it also limits. Writers understand the appeal of a conflicted hero, or a villain with redeeming qualities. We draw our students' attention to the complex characters great writers create and use discussion of these characters to nudge students to a deeper understanding of themselves and the world. *Where the Wild Things Are* (Sendak, 1988) is an enduring classic because Maurice Sendak has delivered such marvelous characters that resonate with readers of all ages. Is Max a bad boy (he chases the dog with a fork and hammers a nail into the wall) or a good one? After all, he is the hero of the book. Can a hero misbehave? And if a hero can misbehave, does that mean we can be naughty and yet still loved?

Questioning the commonplace in texts extends to informational texts that may not include newer information about the lives of historical figures. Founding fathers who owned enslaved people, artists who abused children, and athletes who cheated to win have left behind a complicated legacy for young people to work through. These should not be confused with the flawed or tragic heroes of literature (think Hamlet), but rather perceived as real, accomplished people who also did things that hurt others in material ways.

Questioning Female Gender Roles

The role of Pandora can be used to challenge assumptions about gender in story. In the traditional myth, Pandora is sent to Prometheus as punishment for stealing the fire Zeus forbade him to take. Ninth-grade English teacher Tim Rose used this story in a larger unit on teaching the heroic cycle in literature. He invited his students to question this and other stories of women as sources of annoyance and punishment and asked them to draw comparisons to similar modern figures on television (e.g., countless sitcom mothers-in-law). Several students cited examples of the presence of a "mean girl" character in teen comedy movies who torments others.

Eighth-grade teacher Helena O'Brien teaches her students each year about the Bechdel-Wallace test (https://bechdeltest.com) for representation of women in fiction, named after the writer and artist Alison Bechdel, who called for books and films that featured at least two female characters who talked to each other about subjects other than men. "Each year I pick a book that will be released as a movie," said Ms. O'Brien. This year she paired *Little Women* (Alcott, 2006)

How do we question
the commonplace
in a text?

and *Sisterhood of the Traveling Pants* (Brashares, 2001) to compare and contrast. Both stories describe four very different female characters who are linked by their deep love and respect for one another. However, the historical contexts (the Civil War era vs. the present day) allowed students to compare the similarities and differences between society's expectations of young women. "The Bechdel test is one way I keep the idea of questioning the commonplace in front of them. It's a way to build the habit of looking at gender representations," she said.

Questioning Male Gender Roles

Traditional gender roles are confining for boys as well as girls. Robin Mello's (2001) research on perceptions of gender roles in heroes and heroines found that the fourth-grade boys in her study struggled with accepting a hero in a story who could be strong and caring, even as they expressed anxiety about having to give up their own more gentle behaviors when they became men. Stories invite discussion about traditionally assigned gender roles for boys and girls. Some of our favorites for discussion among elementary readers on the role of boys in literary and informational texts include the following:

- *When the Bees Fly Home* (Andrea Cheng, 2015)

- *Tough Boris* (Mem Fox, 1998)

- *Horace and Morris but Mostly Delores* (James Howe, 2003)

- *Stories for Boys Who Dare to Be Different: True Tales of Amazing Boys Who Changed the World Without Killing Dragons* (Ben Brooks, 2018)

Again, the goal in developing a critical literacy habit among students is not to castigate authors and their works but to understand where these viewpoints may come from and how they are grounded in the context of the time period and the author's viewpoint, such as Louisa May Alcott's portrayal of young females in *Little Women*, which she wrote in 1868. We also use these texts to help our students know themselves and the world a bit better. Mello (2001) reminds us that "when students are presented with a variety of gender roles from disparate cultural texts, they begin to examine their own understanding of how to assign value to gender roles and gendered relationships" (p. 554).

Questioning Power and Class

Like gender issues, power and class issues are easily overlooked by readers unaccustomed to close examination of the commonplace. Students' unquestioned acceptance of power and class relationships can often be found in their own writing. MacGillivray and Martinez conducted a study that will always remain with us on the writing of second graders. One girl's story recounted the tale of a princess who wore a plain dress and did not have a ticket to the ball. Her solution was to commit suicide—"death as a solution to unanswered desire" (1998, p. 54). As teachers, we have seen disconcerting representations of material goods and conformity in our own students' stories—a reminder to us about the pervasiveness of these perceptions.

Fortunately, there are many books that offer ideal opportunities for discussion about social class, social groups, and power in order to address various aspects of economic status. You can begin by asking your students how they "know" someone is wealthy and list their predictable responses—a large house, late-model cars, jewelry, and such. Make a similar list about people who have less money, and they again offer examples related to possessions. Then invite them to describe character traits of the wealthy and poor in the texts they read, and point out the subjective observations they make regarding intelligence, work ethic, and honesty.

Third-grade teacher Valentina Guzman had her students read *The Hundred Dresses* (Estes, 2004) to explore the issue of material possessions. In this moving story, a girl wears the same dress every day to school but tells her classmates that she has 100 dresses at home. After discussing the content, Ms. Guzman asked her students to examine other books in the classroom and sort them according the relative wealth of the main character. Students quickly noticed that most books portrayed a boy or girl living in a suburban, middle class neighborhood, and those set in an urban center usually had a moderate level of possessions. When characters were identified as being poor, they were most commonly African American or Latinx. Ms. Guzman asked her students to write their reactions to this discovery and to propose what they could do to change this. Corazon wrote, "We can make a list of books that do a better job of showing that some people have less money" and offered to send this list to the school librarian.

Questioning of the commonplace is a habit worthy of building. However, the goal is for students to apply this habit to wider reading. Therefore, after raising awareness of issues about the portrayal of socioeconomic status, invite students to examine other books in the classroom as well as popular magazines, news reports, and advertisements. By this point, they are more skilled at asking questions about representations of wealth and power. An observation checklist can be found in Figure 4.3 to track student progress in increasingly complex texts.

> Questioning of the commonplace is a habit worthy of building. However, the goal is for students to apply this habit to wider reading.

Figure 4.3 Observation checklist for questioning the commonplace in text.

Name: _____   Grade/Subject _____

In reading and critiquing literary and informational texts, does the student . . . ?

Question	Date	Name of Text and Quantitative/Qualitative Level	Student Evidence
Identify heroes and villains in a story and tell how the behavior of those characters varies from archetypal behavior			
Identify the roles of men and women and recognize how those roles differ from what might be expected			
Identify ways in which characters treat other characters based on gender or sexual-orientation stereotypes			
Identify ways in which characters treat other characters based on racial or ethnic stereotypes			
Identify ways in which characters treat other characters based on language or religious stereotypes			
Identify ways in which characters treat other characters based on physical, cognitive, or mental-health stereotypes			
Identify the social and/or economic status of characters and recognize how status affects a character's power and how the character is treated by others			

online resources 🔎 Available for download at **resources.corwin.com/comprehension**

Consider the Role of the Author

The habit of critical literacy requires that students ask questions not only about the message but about the author as well. As with so many aspects of the habits of great readers, this is an outgrowth of another comprehension strategy—Questioning the Author (Beck et al., 1996). This approach encourages readers to pose questions they might ask an author if the author were there in the room. ("How did you learn about this topic?" or "Why did you write this book?") You can see the how these questions move readers even closer to asking questions that lead them to evaluate the text. "How did you learn about this topic?" begs another: "Is there other information that you left out of this book?" We think of this as granting readers permission to *doubt*. What a potent gift.

Questioning the Author of a Work of Fiction

Students should be asked to consider the author's motives for writing the text. Rosamie Santos led a discussion with Trina and Valerie, two of her seventh graders, who had just finished Viola Canales's *The Tequila Worm* (2005). This is the story of Sofia, who wins a scholarship to an exclusive boarding school and is confronted with a culture clash of values and mores that differ from those of her childhood community. Ms. Santos asked, "Why might Canales have written this book?" Trina cited the author's dedication to the teachers and staff of a school with a name similar to the one in the book.

"I think she went to boarding school, and she wanted to tell what it was like for her." The girls bandied this idea around for a few minutes, citing examples in the text that would support this conclusion. Nancy then asked them if that meant the book was true.

"Oh, no," answered both of them. Valerie continued, "Besides the fact that you can tell it's a novel because the girl's name is different and all, you can't call it true because it's not called an autobiography. If it said that, then it could be true."

Ms. Santos reminded them about memoirs as a genre. The three of them discussed the controversy about the lack of veracity expected of a memoir, and what an author would need to do in order to make it clear to readers that fictionalized accounts were blended with true events. This led Trina to raise the question about the "based on a

We think of this as granting readers permission to *doubt*. What a potent gift.

How do we consider the role of the author?

true story" taglines on so many movies. "How can you know what's true and what's not?" she asked. "If they tell you to 'write what you know,' how do you know where to draw the line?"

Valerie had a reply for her. "I think it's about looking for other info when you read or when you watch a movie. There's lots of stuff out there about where a story comes from, but you

Informational texts require examining the role of the author, too, and there is perhaps no more important text to do this with than the text found on the internet.

have to know to go look for it." Ms. Santos asked the girls if the author of *The Tequila Worm* would need to omit information. "Well, yeah, sure," answered Valerie. "Like, she can't really write about what the other girls at the boarding school thought of her. She can only describe it the way she sees it."

Questioning the Author of Informational Texts

Informational texts require examining the role of the author, too, and there is perhaps no more important text to do this with than the text found on the internet. When readers apply critical reading strategies to this genre, they ask questions that examine the sources of information the author used to write the text and the role of the author in developing the text. They also consider the purpose for the text and how the author might have obtained the information. The informational texts that our students encounter on the internet often require that our students develop their critical lenses. For example, here's how eighth-grade teacher Dylan Kaminsky used conversation to nudge Jon, a student, to think critically about the information he was reading on the internet.

Jon is a dedicated fan of skateboarding and has been interested in learning more about *parkour*, an aggressive form of athleticism that turns urban landscapes into obstacle courses. Participants use movements influenced by martial arts, gymnastics, and combat training.

Jon consulted Wikipedia for some basic information and learned about the philosophical falling out between the founders of the discipline. Jon's knowledge of this controversy led him to consider his own views of the activity—is it a competitive sport, or an art form? Mr. Kaminsky asked him about his own opinions and discussed the rhetoric he was likely to encounter on the websites. Jon described the kind of boastful talk he hears and uses when skateboarding with others and predicted that some sites might contain language or information that would be insulting or untrue. Jon then read several websites from both points of view and concluded that he was more interested in the technical execution of the moves rather than in competition. He therefore decided to spend his time exploring a website associated with founder David Belle. He has learned how to execute a few basic moves such as wall pops, rolls, and vaults, and is currently perfecting his cat jump. He participates in an online community of parkour enthusiasts in the San Diego area. There's not much available to Jon on parkour in traditional print genre, so his application of critical literacy helps him navigate digital information.

Critical readers who are in the habit of considering the role of the author don't always need to locate the "right" answer, or even seek it out. Rather, readers like Trina and Valerie demonstrate that they are conscious of the hand of the author in the works they read and are comfortable with contemplating the author's influence. Jon's analysis of the various parkour websites he visited began with a quick look at the source. Jon had developed the habit of questioning the role of the author in order to understand and evaluate the information. This awareness of the author not only deepens their understanding of what they read; it also gives them insight into their own lives. An observation checklist for tracking students' growth in considering the author can be found in Figure 4.4.

Seek Alternative Perspectives

The signature of a critical reader is the ability to actively consider alternative perspectives to the one presented in the text. As a reminder, the emphasis is not on a default position that all authors have actively sought to obscure any other perspectives, but rather that every writer adopts a particular lens, and that there may be other viewpoints worth considering as well. In particular, historical and cultural considerations can influence the message of the text.

Figure 4.4 Observation checklist for considering the author's role in text.

Name: _____ Grade/Subject _____

In reading and critiquing literary and informational texts, does the student . . . ?

Question	Date	Text Title and Quantitative/ Qualitative Level	Student Evidence
Identify possible sources of information that an author uses to write a literary or informational text			
Identify material that might be factual in a work of fiction			
Identify material that might be fictional in a work of nonfiction			
Recognize the possible motives that an author might have for writing the text			
Explain how characters represent the author's message			

online resources   Available for download at **resources.corwin.com/comprehension**

This is not an understanding typically assumed by most young readers. Sam Wineburg (1991), the noted historian and educator, found that historians and students differ in the reading of documents in one crucial way—the students did not take into account who wrote it or when it was written. Instead, these "novice historians" took the information at face value and did not understand the implications of authorship and place on writing. He calls this a difference in "epistemological stance" (1991, p. 495); we would attribute it to "uncritical literacy." Either way, this is a troubling finding, especially when one considers the implications. For example, we don't want readers to accept a tree logging company's perspective without also hearing from a botanist (or vice versa). It isn't hyperbole to assert that the ability to seek out multiple perspectives in order to make decisions and take action is at the heart of our democratic process.

> The ability to seek out multiple perspectives in order to make decisions and take action is at the heart of our democratic process.

Now of course, the ways to model multiple perspectives aren't always so serious, especially with younger readers. The intent, rather, is to foster the habit of considering more than one perspective. Primary teachers everywhere use *The True Story of the Three Little Pigs* (Scieszka, 1999) to encourage students to reconsider the traditional fairy tale. The wolf's explanation that "the real story is about a sneeze and a cup of sugar" (p. 6) is slyly humorous and invites readers to notice when the wolf seems to protest too much.

Unearthing multiple perspectives requires effort and a willingness to explore seemingly unconnected information. Eleventh-grade English teacher Lauren Thorpe had taught a unit of study using Hansberry's 1957 play *Raisin in the Sun* as the target text and had provided additional informational readings throughout about the practice of redlining to prevent African American families from buying property. "I wanted to make sure they had a historical record of the context of the play. Background information is really important for them to understand the perspectives of the antagonist and protagonist," said the teacher.

A few weeks after her class had completed the unit, an article about a newly released study caught Ms. Thorpe's attention. The title "Do Housing Vouchers Improve Academic Performance? Evidence from New York City" (Schwartz et al., 2020) intrigued her. "We live in California, where housing disparities are being linked to the rapid rise of homelessness in the state," she said. The state had passed new affordable housing requirements that were roiling some communities, including some in and near her school district. "I did some reading about it, and what really caught my attention was someone's observation that housing policy is education policy," she continued. "I knew I had to find out more, and so did my students."

Ms. Thorpe introduced the idea to her students the following week, noting that she didn't have an answer, but rather new questions. "I never thought about this before," she told her classes. "But I can't help but think about Walter Lee Younger, his mother and his son, Travis [characters from the play]. Can we learn more about it together?" She shared this paragraph from the conclusion of the research article that sparked her inquiry:

> Our results provide compelling evidence that vouchers improve the educational outcomes of low-income students.

These educational benefits should be considered when policymakers weigh the benefits and costs of housing choice vouchers. Further, our results suggest that targeting housing vouchers to households with children might be fruitful for reducing inequality in the short run and, potentially, in the long run. (Schwartz et al., 2020, p. 155)

For the next two weeks, they read portions of the research article, consulted local housing ordinances, and located geospatial data on Google Earth to examine comparative housing growth in their zip codes. "It was amazing to watch," said the teacher. "They organized themselves across class periods so they could share resources. One of my third-period students set up a wiki so they could communicate and curate materials." Inspired by what they learned from their inquiry, they contacted members of the school board, led by a group of students from across Ms. Thorpe's classes . . .

But we're getting ahead of ourselves. You can see the thrill of reading comprehension taking shape right before your eyes in this English teacher's classes. The transformation from adopting a critical literacy lens to taking action can happen quickly. That thrill of asking oneself "What does this text inspire me to do?" is at the nexus of what reading can do for heart, mind, and soul. We will return to the actions Ms. Thorpe's class took later in this chapter. In the meantime, the willingness to take on other perspectives is crucial for critique. Figure 4.5 provides an observation checklist to track evidence of this with your students.

> That thrill of asking oneself "What does this text inspire me to do?" is at the nexus of what reading can do for heart, mind, and soul.

Goal Setting Through Student-Generated Questions

Our daily lives are goal driven. Some goals are to meet basic needs of food, shelter, and safety, while others are social and concern personal and professional relationships. Resolutions aside, however, most of us don't formally write out the goals we have for ourselves, even as we monitor our health data, financial records, and overall well-being (e.g., spending time with family and friends). There has been increased attention to setting goals with students as a means for setting purposes for learning and signaling what success looks like. The use of success criteria with learners has been demonstrated as being of considerable value. With an effect size of 0.54, success criteria influence student learning at a significant level

Figure 4.5 Observation checklist for seeking other perspectives through text.

Name: _____ Grade/Subject _____

In reading and critiquing literary and informational texts, does the student . . . ?

Question	Date	Text Title(s) and Quantitative/ Qualitative Level	Student Evidence
Identify the perspectives of different characters in a text			
Recount the narrative from another character's perspective			
Explain the historical or cultural influences on a text			
Compare and contrast alternative perspectives between texts			
Recognize bias demonstrated by a person in a book or by the author of a text			
Recognize the harm bias causes others			
Identify gaps in information in a text and explain how to learn more			

 Available for download at **resources.corwin.com/comprehension**

(Hattie Ranking, n.d.). The raised level of awareness of success criteria has resulted in lots more conversation about learning goals with students, and that's a good thing. Goals such as Tre's at the beginning of this chapter (reading all the Lemony Snicket books) are pretty straightforward to measure. But some goals are a bit harder to articulate, especially when you aren't quite sure where the learning is going to take you. For instance, it would be difficult to list at the outset the goals of Ms. Thorpe's inquiry about housing policy. When it comes to topics like this that are less well defined, having a process in place to create student-generated questions is useful.

Fostering Creative Thinking

Self-questioning is necessary to reading critically and can be supported by giving students opportunities to do so individually and collectively. This cognitive habit is what fuels creativity and curiosity, but unfortunately in practice, self-questioning does not occur frequently in schools. Brookhart (2013) notes that creativity is not synonymous with being "clever, humorous, artistically pleasing, enthusiastic, or persuasive" but rather reflects the following characteristics of a student (p. 32):

- Recognizes the importance of a deep knowledge base and continually works to learn new things

- Is open to new ideas and actively seeks them out

- Finds source material in a wide variety of media, people, and events

- Organizes and reorganizes ideas into different categories or combinations and then evaluates whether the results are interesting, new, or helpful

- Uses trial and error when unsure how to proceed, viewing failure as an opportunity to learn

Figure 4.6 provides an approach to assessing creativity in students' work.

These skills and dispositions are exactly the kind of thing we are trying to develop in our students every day. That is, they are acquiring not just the skill of reading, but also the willingness to engage with texts and use them as a path to achieve something new. As students read critically, they begin to formulate possible questions that help them answer the question: "What does this text inspire me to do?" Having said that, this question goes unvoiced and unanswered unless we create the space for it to breathe.

Think-Outside-the-Box Questions

Questions created by students, not by the teacher, can result in deep learning. In addition, the quality of the questions students generate

> This cognitive habit is what fuels creativity and curiosity, but unfortunately in practice, self-questioning does not occur frequently in schools.

> Questions created by students, not by the teacher, can result in deep learning.

Figure 4.6 Assessing creativity.

	Very Creative	Creative	Ordinary/Routine	Imitative
Variety of ideas and contexts	Ideas represent a startling variety of important concepts from different contexts or disciplines	Ideas represent important concepts from different contexts or disciplines	Ideas represent important concepts from the same or similar contexts or disciplines	Ideas do not represent important concepts
Variety of sources	Created product draws on a wide variety of sources, including different texts, media, resource persons, or personal experiences	Created product draws on a variety of sources, including different texts, media, resource persons, or personal experiences	Created product draws on a limited set of sources and media	Created product draws on only one source or on sources that are not trustworthy or appropriate
Combining ideas	Ideas are combined in original and surprising ways to solve a problem, address an issue, or make something new	Ideas are combined in original ways to solve a problem, address an issue, or make something new	Ideas are combined in ways that are derived from the thinking of others (for example, of the authors in sources consulted)	Ideas are copied or restated from the sources consulted
Communicating something new	Created product is interesting, new, or helpful, making an original contribution that includes identifying a previously unknown problem, issue, or purpose	Created product is interesting, new, or helpful, making an original contribution for its intended purpose (for example, solving a problem or addressing an issue)	Created product serves its intended purpose (for example, solving a problem or addressing an issue)	Created product does not serve its intended purpose (for example, solving a problem or addressing an issue)

Source: Brookhart, S. M. (2013). *How to create and use rubrics for formative assessment and grading,* p. 54. ASCD. Copyright 2013 by ASCD. Adapted with permission.

provides insight into how much they comprehend of the text. In order to generate questions, students must consider what knowledge they already have about a subject and apply that knowledge in new and novel ways. In fact, this is the definition of transfer of learning: the ability to utilize knowledge in situations that are unique and previously unrehearsed (Bransford et al., 2000). The flowchart in Figure 4.7 is a visual representation of what King (1992) has called think-outside-the-box questions. The purpose of these questions is to illustrate a process for how students can make decisions about formulating a plan for taking action.

Transfer of learning: the ability to utilize knowledge in situations that are unique and previously unrehearsed

Figure 4.7 Think-outside-the-box questions.

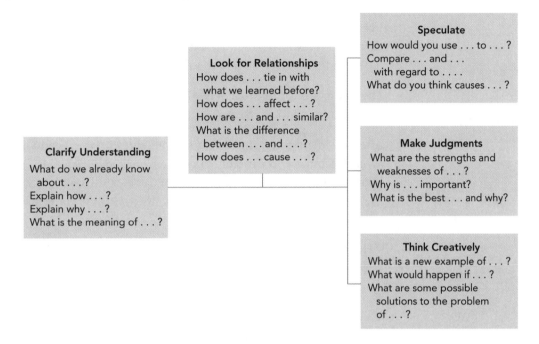

Source: Adapted from King, A. (1992). Facilitating elaborative learning through guided student-generated questioning. p. 122. *Educational Psychologist, 27*(11), 111–126. Used by permission of Lawrence A. Erlbaum Associates.

The intention is not to choose from a list of questions, but rather to pose sets of questions for students to wrestle with as they move toward action. Therefore, this should be considered a map of the process, rather than a rigid sequence. Second-grade teacher Bethany Ford-Robinson used a version of this process to help her students address an issue they had learned about through their readings about food deserts in some urban communities. But as residents of a small town in a sparsely populated area of the country, they recognized that their own community was becoming a food desert. "The last grocery store in our town closed a few months ago, and now people have to make a 30-mile round trip to go to get fresh food," said the teacher. "What we have now is a small convenience store here in town, but it mostly sells processed food."

Her students began the process as a whole class, beginning with a chart titled List What We Know (*clarifying their understanding*).

"This is the time when we list what we already know about the problem. Let's make a list," said Ms. Ford-Robinson. As the children talked, she wrote their facts on chart paper, at times asking them follow-up questions. "Tell us what you mean when you talk about 'no fresh food,' Riley. What are some examples?"

The boy answered immediately. "Like tomatoes. I like tomatoes, but it's too far to go to get them."

After several minutes, she moved her students into the second phase, What Is Similar and Different? (*looking for relationships*). "I try to get them to this point as quickly as I can," she said later. "Otherwise, they get stuck in talking about what they already know without moving forward."

 "How does what has happened in our town relate to what we've already learned?" the teacher asked.

The children discussed the idea of a food desert, and when asked about similarities and differences, Jenna said, "One difference is that we have lots of land here, and in some of the cities they didn't."

"And something that's the same is we don't have lots of bees either. My papa was telling me there's problems with things growing when there's not lotsa bees 'round," Dominic added.

"And they don't get tomatoes," Riley said, "just like we don't get 'em either."

When the chart was full, Ms. Ford-Robinson tore it off and fastened it next to the first one. For the next 15 minutes, they moved through the next two steps of the process: We Wonder (*speculating*) and Importance (*judgments*). Each component of the decision-making process had its own chart. The teacher then summarized and reviewed the class's thinking to that point.

"Now comes the most fun. What Ideas do we have (*thinking creatively*)?" For this phase, she moved students into small groups, each with their own chart paper and markers. Each group came up with ideas for what they could do and then shared them with the rest of the class. Several groups had come up with ideas about growing vegetables, which served as a place of consensus. Ms. Ford-Robinson suggested that they might be able to grow vegetables on the grounds of the school. (The school's parent-teacher organization had proposed a similar idea at the previous month's meeting).

With the aid of several school and community groups, a community garden was born. Although it would be overstating it to say that this second-grade class was the starting point, the children sparked discussion among other adults about possibilities. Three years later, Ms. Ford-Robinson's classroom has a special charge. They start the seedling plants for all the tomatoes grown in the school's community garden.

Taking Action

The drive to take action emanates from the level of comprehension students have for the text as well as the motivation and engagement that compels them to learn more. Not all of their actions need to culminate with a community garden, of course. Rather, we hope that students are regularly challenged to do something with the knowledge they've gained. It comes down to this: *What does the text inspire one to do?* There are a number of choices teachers can offer, from research and writing to presenting or debating.

Consider the group of kindergarten students who had read, with their teacher, *The Day the Crayons Quit* (Daywalt, 2013). Their teacher asked them what they were inspired to do, following several readings over the week, in which they focused on vocabulary and the perspective of different characters, all crayons. One group of students decided to search the internet to figure out the correct color of the sun. (The picture book includes a debate about this.) Another group wanted to know if the author had written other books (he had not at the time) and went on a search for additional books about crayons specifically and art in general. Still another group decided to write their own books about what their crayons would say. And one student wrote a book about what her shoes might argue about. Each student was inspired, but not in the same way as everyone else in the class. This served to reinforce the idea that reading allows you to do something with the ideas that you gain from the experience.

Richard Anderson, an eminent scholar in reading research, speaks of students being more than consumers of information. Instead, he

> The drive to take action emanates from the level of comprehension students have for the text as well as the motivation and engagement that compels them to learn more.

> Richard Anderson proposes that we help our students become *storytellers*, *informers*, and *arguers*.

proposes that we help our students become *storytellers, informers*, and *arguers* (personal communication, June 18, 2019). Notice how these parallel the three major types of writing we ask students to produce. Narrative texts tell stories, both real and imagined. Informational texts are used to build knowledge using factual information. And argumentative texts are written to propose claims and address counterclaims using rhetorical structures.

Storytellers can take action by acting out a skit, writing poetry, or conveying a personal narrative about a part of their own life, to name just a few. Jerome Thornton's seventh-grade students read Kwame Alexander's open verse story *The Crossover* (2015) as part of a unit on award-winning books, and many liked the structure and the storyline. Mr. Thornton recognized the enthusiasm and proposed that his students spend an additional week extending the work. "I gave them several options, such as writing their own story using Alexander's technique, producing a report on the author, or creating a tableau of a key scene." One group of Mr. Thornton's students produced a short video enacting a key scene between the twin brothers that represented a major conflict in the book. The video was such a hit that the students showed it in all of Mr. Thornton's classes. "They [the students] kick-started the creative juices," he said. "I've had several other student groups make videos about other books we're reading."

How do we encourage action through comprehension?

Informers can take action by producing knowledge that reaches others. The kindergartners at Slash Pine Elementary School compose class letters to classes in other grades about what they are learning. Diana Ortez, one of the kindergarten teachers, explained that every month her class sets up a tour of their classroom for other classes to visit. "Last month we studied light in science. The students made shadow boxes to demonstrate the effects of light on objects, drew posters about how light from the sun hits the earth and moon, and had a demonstration about prisms" she said. The kindergarten students served as docents for the visitors to explain what they knew about light. "These actually don't take very long to do," said Ms. Ortiz. "I've done all these experiments for years with my kids, but them knowing they would be replicating these for an audience took their learning to a new level. Plus, it really boosted their academic language skills."

The students in Ms. Thorpe's 11th-grade English class who learned about housing policies and their relationship to academic achievement took on the collective role of arguers. They learned in reading the research on the subject that the researchers determined that the rise in reading and math levels for New York City students whose families who received housing vouchers didn't come because they changed schools. (Few did.) Rather, it was, in the words of Schwartz and her colleagues, due to "lessening rent burdens," thereby "stabilizing families" (2020, p. 131). After gathering additional information about local housing conditions, Ms. Thorpe's students met with the administration and the parent-teacher organization at the school to present what they had learned. "The PTO was a catalyst for this," said Ms. Thorpe. With their backing, students contacted members of the school board and got on the agenda. "They asked the school board to petition in city council to reexamine their current housing voucher policies." This isn't a finished story, but rather a beginning. The students' efforts have mobilized key stakeholders in the community to consider public policy. That's no small accomplishment.

The students in Marla Hampson's second-grade class were studying Johnny Appleseed. Working with her library media specialist, Ms. Hampson collected a number of books that provided information about Johnny Appleseed. Students were provided options about which texts they would read. Some students selected texts that caused them to struggle, and Ms. Hampson reminded them about their rights as readers, which include abandoning a text with reason. She also noted that they could get help from others if the words were complicated or if they were not sure about some of the sentences.

Each day, students were invited to select a text to read, either as part of their after-school program or at home. As students' background knowledge grew, so did their ability to read more complex texts. They also noted similarities between texts and areas where the information seemed to contradict. As second grader Javier said, "Not everything about him is true. There are some stories that are made up to make him more important. But he did some good things that helped people."

Ms. Hampson used the three roles described by Anderson to inspire her students. As she explained,

> When we finish all of our reading about Johnny Appleseed, you'll have some choices. You might want to be a storyteller.

That's a person who uses true information, like the information from the books we've read, and then adds information to make the story come alive. Not all of the information has to be historically true. You can use your imagination to write dialogue. But it has to be reasonable. It would not be reasonable to say that Johnny Appleseed was captured by aliens or that he sailed to America on the *Titanic*. Storytellers provide us with information, and they help us imagine the experience.

Ms. Hampson continued,

Or you could be an informer. Informers stick to the facts. They teach us things that matter, and they make sure that we understand the who, what, where, when, why, and how of the information. They make sure that they explain it in a way that we can remember. Informing a younger sister, brother, or cousin is different from informing Ms. Jimenez, the school librarian. Informers need to know a lot of stuff, because people like to ask explainers questions.

And finally, Ms. Hampson explained the arguer.

You can also be an arguer. But you have to start with something that is not simply a fact. It wouldn't be very effective to argue that Johnny planted grapes or corn. Arguers select topics that have some controversy or differences in ideas. Arguers have an opinion, and they provide reasons for that opinion. They try to get the rest of us to agree.

The students in Ms. Hampson's class selected from these three roles and knew that they would have time the week following their readings about Johnny Appleseed to share with their groups. They were inspired to reread texts, take notes, collect information, and prepare for the experience the following week. They became active producers and selected their roles carefully. And in doing so, they better comprehended the texts they were reading.

Taking Accurate and Ethical Action

The work accomplished by Ms. Thorpe's 11th-grade students (now activists) required them to be able to accurately synthesize information in order to extend it in a new and creative way. Synthesis is often thought of as being a reading comprehension skill, but it can be the pathway to taking action. However, there must be integrity in what students do with the information they gather, especially if they are integrating information from many sources.

iStock.com/valentinrussanov

Synthesis is often thought of as being a reading comprehension skill, but it can be the pathway to taking action.

If the information is conveyed incorrectly, or if information is missing, then the resultant action suffers. Shanahan proposes that we reconsider how it is that synthesis is considered across a continuum of expression at six levels (personal communication, January 5, 2020):

1. From no information drawn from sources ⟷ To lots of information drawn from sources.

2. From information drawn from one source ⟷ To information drawn from multiple sources.

3. From information used, but inaccurately ⟷ To information used accurately.

4. From information drawn from sources in a discrete manner ⟷ To information drawn from sources that is combined, compared, and coordinated.

5. From information used, but not sourced ⟷ To information that is used, and the source of the information is cited

6. From information used inappropriately (the source information is accurate, but does not support the writers/speakers' point) ⟷ To information that is used appropriately.

All the creativity in the world doesn't matter if information is not used in ways that are credible, accurate, ethical, and astute.

But all the creativity in the world doesn't matter if information is not used in ways that are credible, accurate, ethical, and astute. The use of information to activate the construction of new and novel responses is balanced by whether the results are themselves credible, accurate, ethical, and astute. The work students produce should

1. *Expand their current knowledge.* Students who find authors whose words resonate, and then are determined to find out what else those writers have produced, are expanding their knowledge.

2. *Enhance relationships*, as when the kindergartners invited other classes to see what they had learned.

3. *Build connections across differences*, as when the third-grade students examined books in their classroom for portrayals of power and class and developed a list of books for their school librarian to consider adding to the collection.

4. *Create new opportunities to act on knowledge*, as with the 11th graders who petitioned city council about housing voucher policies.

In doing so, they tap into all the domains of language necessary to build reading comprehension skills. Their oral language skills develop each time they explain, recount, share, and debate. Their listening skills are enhanced as well, as they process, understand, formulate, empathize, and reflect. Perhaps most important of all is that their thinking skills develop. In the process of reading and talking about their reading, they construct ideas, make connections to other ideas, plan, and create.

Conclusion

As we noted at the outset of this book, the point of comprehension is no longer just comprehension. We want students to take action on the world—to do something that matters—because they have read and understood texts. We hope that students become informed decision makers who carefully consider information and who take ethical action. Of course, they need skills in comprehension to do so.

And they need to be motivated to engage in a wide range of reading tasks. But we should not limit students' learning to the skills of comprehension and then try to manipulate them into reading. Instead, the experiences students have in school should traverse the *skill*, *will*, and *thrill* landscape such that they read more and better, and make the world a little better because they are in it.

5

Tools for Reading Comprehension Instruction

In 1995, *Discover* magazine published an account of a railroad worker who survived a significant brain injury. Here's the opening paragraph of the article (Shreeve, 1995, p. 79):

> Attend the tale of Phineas Gage. Honest, well-liked by friends and fellow workers on the Rutland and Burlington Railroad, Gage was a young man of exemplary character and promise until one day in September 1848. While tamping down the blasting powder for a dynamite charge, Gage inadvertently sparked an explosion. The inch-thick tamping rod rocketed through his cheek, obliterating his left eye on its way through his brain and out the top of his skull. The rod landed several yards away, and Gage fell back in a convulsive heap. Yet a moment later he stood up and spoke; his fellow workers watched, aghast, then drove him by oxcart to a hotel, where a local doctor, one John Harlow, dressed his wounds. As Harlow stuck his index fingers into the holes in Gage's face and head until their tips met, the young man inquired when he would be able to return to work.

Consider for a moment the comprehension skills you used to understand this paragraph. There were a number of them, right? You had to decode the words, read them quickly enough to make meaning, and mobilize your background knowledge and vocabulary understanding. Further, you did these things automatically, without devoting a lot of conscious thought to your processes.

Now ask yourself a different question: If you were to use this passage with your students, which components would you teach? The text holds the potential for any number of possibilities: comprehension strategies, vocabulary, text structure, or text features (there's an illustration of the injury in the original text), to name a few. Your choice of what to teach will be informed by the content and language standards you're focused on at the time, the needs of your students as noted in formative assessments, and your knowledge of students' current skills and knowledge. Again, there isn't one "right" decision for this text. Like most, it offers a range of possibilities.

In one classroom, we observed a teacher model and think aloud using visualizing and historical context for this first paragraph. She explained the mental images she had of the world in 1848, the type of transportation offered, and the rudimentary knowledge of the medical profession at the time. In another classroom, we saw a teacher lead a small group discussion on word-solving approaches. Her students were applying their analysis of context clues and word parts in particular to figure out the unfamiliar vocabulary, such as *tamping, obliterating, convulsive,* and *aghast.* In still another classroom, we witnessed a teacher coordinating collaborative groups as they used text structure clues to form a prediction about what the author would explain next.

Skilled readers are able to consolidate strategies and activate them at appropriate times in service of comprehension—a marker of transfer of learning.

In all three cases, students were developing a mental model they could use later to read the entire article. Their teachers understood that fostering comprehension was critical to the development of skilled readers who could apply literacy strategies in authentic situations. And in all three cases, these teachers knew that explaining or modeling or discussing had to be connected with other tasks. These teachers know that skilled readers are able to consolidate strategies and activate them at appropriate times in service of comprehension—a marker of transfer of learning.

There's no untangling the considerations of texts and tasks in teaching for comprehension. After all, reading comprehension doesn't occur in a vacuum. There is no reading comprehension without a text, of course. Further, reading a text in school occurs within the instructional milieu. If the text alone were sufficient, then it would be enough to seat children in a library and call it a day. But the text alone, no matter how rich with potential, is wasted in the face of ineffective instruction. The RAND Reading Study Group stated as much in their 2002 report about comprehension, noting that the text, the activity, and the context can either enhance or inhibit understanding. In this chapter, we examine the tools of our trade, namely, the texts we utilize and the instruction and accompanying tasks we design to promote students' reading comprehension. These tasks are driven by the instructional moves we use and are selected based on an understanding of what the text has to offer.

> If the text alone were sufficient, then it would be enough to seat children in a library and call it a day.

Let us say this upfront: This chapter is dense. We provide a lot of detailed and complex information about text complexity and high-quality instruction. You may want to skim over some of this information and focus on specific needs. Or you may be very interested in the ways in which the selected text impacts comprehension and want to learn more about text complexity. But just know that we know this is complex and less nuanced that the other chapters in this book.

Texts as Tools for Fostering Comprehension

Texts are objects that can be "read," which is to say that they carry information understood by others (Bakhtin, 1981). In the broadest sense of the term, text includes the clothes we choose to wear to show that we are a teachers, the traffic signs we use to get to work, and the physical classroom layout we design to signal to our students how learning occurs in the space. More specifically, texts in a school context comprise the literary, informational, and argumentative works we utilize every day in our teaching. They are a key tool in our teaching toolkit.

Texts are central to comprehension and come in several formats. The most common are print materials, including trade books, textbooks, and articles. The development of technologies has made digital texts ubiquitous in classrooms. Many print and digital texts

There has been a growing appreciation of visual text and its effects on a viewer's comprehension.

are engineered for classroom use, although primary source materials and readings originally intended for a different audience are also used. In addition, there has been a growing appreciation of visual text and its effects on a viewer's comprehension. Visual texts include picture books, graphic novels, and multimedia presentations. The use of color, symbols, shape, and—in the case of video—sound, lighting, and movement are used to convey meaning beyond the textual cues.

Educators consider the characteristics of print and digital texts across several factors. The level of a text may be measured using quantitative or qualitative measures that are arranged in a hierarchical system to predict the relative challenge it will pose. These are approximations, and while they are based on the developmental characteristics of readers at various ages, they cannot account for every individual's strengths, interests, and needs. That said, text readability and text complexity measures provide a good starting point for making decisions about the nature of the texts we use.

Text Readability and Text Complexity

The vocabulary we use in the field to discuss texts can be somewhat confusing, and in those confusions lie misunderstandings that lead to flawed decisions about access. Therefore, we will start by taking on two terms that seem to get tangled together: *text readability* and *text complexity*. While related to each other, they are not synonymous. We will start with readability, since this is the more straightforward of the two.

Text Readability: The Quantitative Measures

The readability of a text is determined by the surface characteristics of the text itself and is quantitative in nature. When you see a number printed on the cover of a book, it is likely derived from a readability formula. There are many such formulas, each with a slightly different algorithm. That said, these are calculated at the word, sentence, and text levels:

- Average number of words per sentence (a proxy for demand on working memory)

- Average number of syllables per sentence (a proxy for the frequency of multisyllabic words)

- Number of different words in a selection (a proxy for relative repeatability and presence of context clues)

- Percentage of rare words compared to a grade-level list or corpus of words (a proxy for the challenge a text might present to a reader of a particular age)

Text readability and text complexity

Readability formulas afford several advantages. The first is that they can be used to calculate characteristics that are not immediately apparent, as most are done by computers. A second advantage is that they provide educators with a calibrated way to discuss texts, rather than vague notions of "grade-level texts," which vary widely even within a school or district. To a more limited extent, they also partially consider the relative difficulty of the text for a reader, at least in making a reasonable estimation of known words and related concepts. Finally, many readability formulas are easy to use and widely available on free internet websites and within word processing software. Documents written in Microsoft Word, for example, can report a Flesch Reading Ease Score, which is on a 100-point scale. The higher the score, the easier it is to read. The program also generates a self-explanatory Flesch-Kincaid Grade Level Score. Other programs are proprietary, such as the well-known Lexile and ATOS text readability measures. While you can't directly calculate these scores, there are extensive lists of published texts and their measures (see Figure 5.1 for an overview of common quantitative measures).

The problem with a sole reliance on a readability measure is that it is not geared to detecting the nuances of a text.

The problem with a sole reliance on a readability measure is that it is not geared to detecting the nuances of a text. Consider this sentence: "It was a bright cold day in April, and the clocks were striking thirteen." From a readability standpoint, it is pretty easy. It is composed of 14 words, all of which are on the Dolch sight word list for primary readers. Only three of those words have two syllables, while the

Figure 5.1 Summary of quantitative text measures.

Name	Purpose	Factors Used	Ease of Use	Notes
Fry Readability Formula	Assesses text difficulty	Sentence length and syllables	Easy; use graph	Primary–college
Flesch-Kincaid Grade-Level Score	Assesses text difficulty	Sentence length and syllables	Easy; use word processing software	K–12
Flesch Reading-Ease Score	Assesses text difficulty	Sentence length and syllables	Easy; use word processing software	Reports relative ease of reading for students in Grade 5–college
Advantage-TASA Open Standard (ATOS)	Assesses text difficulty	Words per sentence, grade level of words, and character length across entire text	Easy; free online calculator and extensive published booklist	Factors fiction/nonfiction and length of text into score
Degrees of Reading Power (DRP)	Assesses text difficulty and reader skills using same scale	Sentence length and relative word frequency	Hard; proprietary software	Designed as criterion-referenced measure for use in grades 1–12
TextEvaluator	Assesses text difficulty and identifies problematic areas	Vocabulary and sentence structures	Hard; uploaded text must meet all requirements	Considers a range of factors that impact comprehension
Lexile Scale	Assesses text difficulty and reader skills using same scale	Sentence length and relative word frequency	Hard; proprietary software Easy; searchable database	Scale is normed for each grade level, starting with Grade 2.
Coh-Metrix	Assesses texts on 64 indices, including measures of text cohesion, linguistic elements, and parsers	Parsers, propositions, and latent semantic analysis, as well as traditional readability measures	Easy; use online calculator	Reports require a high degree of technical knowledge to interpret

Source: Fisher, D., Frey, N., & Lapp, D. (2016). *Text complexity*, p. 39. Corwin.

others have a single syllable each. And yet you might recognize this as the opening sentence of George Orwell's dystopian classic *Nineteen Eighty-Four: A Novel,* written in 1949. The author ably communicates a sense of dissonance in the first line, something a readability formula would not pick up. Rather, your analysis reflected your ability to discern a deeper complexity of this sentence.

Text Complexity

The quantitative measures that calculate readability are primarily performed by machines, but it usually takes a human to figure out the qualitative aspects of a text. These, along with the characteristics of the reader and the task, influence a text's complexity. In this regard, it is relative. A technical report on water quality is less complex for an environmental scientist than it is for a resident of the community that uses the water. A passage about photosynthesis is less complex for a high school biology student than it is for a third-grade science student. This is partially due to the characteristics of the reader but also because of some textual elements. Whether the text is literary or informational, four dimensions of the text should be qualitatively examined:

- Levels of meaning and purpose
- Structure
- Language conventionality and clarity
- Knowledge demands

These qualitative determinations draw on your judgement as a teacher and assist you in making text decisions in a more sophisticated manner.

Qualitative Characteristics of the Text

Beyond the surface structures of a text, which lend themselves to quantitative analysis, lie factors that must be considered more closely. These factors work together to render a text more or less complex. Keep in mind that we are not yet addressing a third consideration—the reader. Having said that, these four factors are useful in delving more systematically, rather than impressionistically. We have developed two qualitative text analysis scales (one for literary text and another for informational text) to further organize these factors. These should not be viewed as being scientifically calibrated, but rather as a way to examine a text in a systematic manner. These scales can be found in Figures 5.2 and 5.3.

Qualitative
characteristics
of texts

Figure 5.2 Qualitative scale of literary texts.

Score	1 point (comfortable)	2 points (grade level)	3 points (stretch)
	Texts that are comfortable and/or build background, fluency, and skills	Texts that require grade-appropriate skills	Texts that would stretch a reader and/or require instruction
Levels of Meaning and Purpose			
Density and Complexity	Single and literal levels of meaning; meaning is explicitly stated	Single but more complex or abstract meaning; some meanings are stated, while others are left to the reader to identify	Significant density and complexity, with multiple levels of meaning; meanings may be more ambiguous
Figurative Language	Limited use of symbolism, metaphors, and poetic language that allude to other unstated concepts; language is explicit and relies on literal interpretations	Figurative language such as imagery, metaphors, symbolism, and personification is used to make connections within the text to more explicit information, and readers are supported in understanding these language devices through examples and explanations	Figurative language plays a significant role in identifying the meaning of the text; more sophisticated figurative language is used (irony and satire, allusions, archaic or less familiar symbolism); the reader is left to interpret these meanings
Purpose	Purpose or main idea is directly and explicitly stated at the beginning of the reading	Purpose is implied but is easily identified based on title or context	Purpose is deliberately withheld from the reader, who must use other interpretative skills to identify it
Structure			
Genre	Genre is familiar, and the text is consistent with the elements of that genre	Genre is unfamiliar, but the text is a reasonable example of that genre, *or* genre is familiar, but text bends and expands the rules for the genre	Genre is unfamiliar, and text bends and expands the rules for the genre
Organization	Organization is conventional, sequential, or chronological, with clear signals and transitions to lead the reader through a story, process, or set of concepts	Organization adheres to most conventions but digresses on occasion to temporarily shift the reader's focus to another point of view, event, time, or place, before returning to the main idea or topic	Organization distorts time or sequence in a deliberate effort to delay the reader's full understanding of the plot, process, or set of concepts; may include significant flashbacks, foreshadowing, or shifting perspectives
Narration	Third-person omniscient narration or an authoritative and credible voice provides an appropriate level of detail and keeps little hidden from the view of the reader	Third-person limited or first-person narration provides accurate, but limited, perspectives or viewpoints	Unreliable narrator provides a distorted or limited view to the reader; the reader must use other clues to deduce the truth; multiple narrators provide conflicting information; shifting points of view keep the reader guessing

Text Features and Graphics	Text features (e.g., bold and italicized words, headings and subheadings) organize information explicitly and guide the reader; graphics or illustrations may be present but are not necessary to understand the main part of the text	Wider array of text features includes margin notes, diagrams, graphs, font changes, and other devices that compete for the reader's attention; graphics and visuals are used to augment and illustrate information in the main part of the text	Limited use of text features to organize information and guide the reader; information in the graphics is not repeated in the main part of the text but is essential for understanding the text
Language Conventionality and Clarity			
Standard English and Variations	Language closely adheres to the reader's linguistic base	Some distance exists between the reader's linguistic base and the language conventions used in the text; the vernacular used is unfamiliar to the reader	The text includes significant and multiple styles of English and its variations, and these are unfamiliar to the reader
Register	Register is casual and familiar	Register is consultative or formal and may be academic but acknowledges the developmental level of the reader	Archaic, formal, domain-specific, or scholarly register
Knowledge Demands			
Background Knowledge	The text contains content that closely matches the reader's life experiences	There is distance between the reader's experiences and those in the text, but there is acknowledgment of these divergent experiences and sufficient explanation to bridge these gaps	The text places demands on the reader that extend far beyond the reader's experiences, and provides little in the way of explanation of these divergent experiences
Prior Knowledge	Prior knowledge needed to understand the text is familiar, and draws on a solid foundation of practical, general, and academic learning	Subject-specific knowledge is required, but the text augments this with review or summary of this information	Specialized or technical content knowledge is presumed, and little in the way of review or explanation of these concepts is present in the text
Cultural Knowledge	The reader uses familiar cultural templates to understand the text; limited or familiar intertextuality	Text primarily references contemporary and popular culture to anchor explanations for new knowledge; intertextuality is used more extensively but is mostly familiar to the reader	Text relies on extensive or unfamiliar intertextuality, and uses artifacts and symbols that reference archaic or historical cultures
Vocabulary Knowledge	Vocabulary is controlled and uses the most commonly held meanings; multiple-meaning words are used in a limited fashion	Vocabulary draws on domain-specific, general academic, and multiple-meaning words, with text supports to guide the reader's correct interpretations of their meanings; the vocabulary used represents familiar concepts and ideas	Vocabulary demand is extensive, domain specific, and representative of complex ideas; the text offers little in the way of context clues to support the reader

Source: Fisher, D., Frey, N., & Lapp, D. (2016). *Text complexity*, pp. 47–49 Corwin.

Figure 5.3 Qualitative scale of informational texts.

Score	1 point (comfortable) Texts that are comfortable and/or build background, fluency, and skills	2 points (grade level) Texts that require grade-appropriate skills	3 points (stretch) Texts that would stretch a reader and/or require instruction
Levels of Meaning and Purpose			
Density and Complexity	Single and literal levels of meaning are present; meaning is explicitly stated.	Multiple layers of specific content are present. Some information must be inferred or integrated with previous content.	Significant density and complexity, with multiple layers of content topics, are present. The reader is expected to critique or evaluate information.
Analogies and Abstract Comparisons	There is limited use of analogous statements. Language relies on literal interpretations.	Analogies and metaphors are used to help the reader make connections between new concepts and the reader's knowledge. These associations draw on familiar processes and phenomena.	The metaphors and analogies used are more abstract and require sophistication and depth of knowledge from the reader. The process or phenomenon used to make a comparison itself requires prior knowledge.
Purpose	The purpose is directly and explicitly stated at the beginning of the text and is in evidence throughout the text.	The text serves both explicit and implicit purposes, which become evident with close inspection of the text.	The text may involve multiple purposes, some of which may be implicit; it requires the reader to critically analyze across texts to discern implicit purposes.
Structure			
Genre	The text exemplifies conventional characteristics of one familiar genre.	The text exemplifies one genre but deviates from typical characteristics of that genre.	The text is presented as being in a specific genre, but it includes other embedded genres.
Organization	One conventional organizational pattern predominates throughout the text. Signal words and phrases are overt and numerous.	More than one conventional organization pattern is included in the text. Signal words and phrases are present.	The text may include a variety of conventional organizational patterns, which are dictated by text content but with little notification or guidance to the reader.
Text Features	The text contains familiar access features such as a table of contents, headings/subheadings, a glossary, and an index.	The text contains conventional access features but also includes detailed information in sidebars, insets, and bulleted lists.	The text contains access features that require the reader to integrate extratextual information, such as preface/prologue, afterword/epilogue, and author/illustrator notes.

Graphic Elements	The text contains familiar graphic elements such as simple diagrams, maps, timelines, photographs, and illustrations with captions. Graphic elements repeat information in the text.	The text contains graphic elements that require interpretation, such as graphs and tables, scale diagrams, and webs. Graphic elements have additional information that supplements the text.	The text contains graphic elements that are less familiar to students and require interpretation, such as cross sections, cutaways, and range and flow maps. Graphic elements have information that complements and is integrated with text.
Language Conventionality and Clarity			
Language Level	The language used is appropriate to the developmental and experiential level of the student.	There is some distance between the text language and the developmental and experiential language level of the student.	The text language uses language conventions and structures unfamiliar to the student, especially those that reflect voices found in specific content areas.
Register	The register is casual and familiar. Humorous language may be used throughout to engage the reader in the information.	The register is consultative or formal, and may be academic, but acknowledges the developmental level of the reader. Humorous or casual language may be used in titles and headings/subheadings.	The register is domain specific, formal, and/or scholarly.
Voice	Information in the text is presented in a straightforward way. Text may use second-person language and a personal tone to draw the reader into the text.	Vocabulary and diction invite the reader's curiosity about the text content while presenting information with an authoritative tone.	Strong authoritative voice dominates the text. Text language is used to impart knowledge to the reader and makes little effort to engage the reader on a personal level.
Knowledge Demands			
Background Knowledge	The content closely matches the reader's primary lived experiences and secondary experiences gained through other media.	The content represents a distance between the reader's primary and secondary experiences, but the text provides explanations to bridge the gap between what is known and unknown.	The content demands specialized knowledge beyond the primary and secondary experiences of the reader and provides no bridge or scaffolding between known and unknown.
Prior Knowledge	Prior knowledge is needed to understand the text, which is familiar and draws on a solid foundation of practical, general, and academic learning.	Subject-specific knowledge is required but is augmented with review or summary of information.	Specialized or technical content knowledge is presumed; little review or explanation of these concepts is present in the text.
Vocabulary Knowledge	The vocabulary is controlled and uses the most commonly held meanings; multiple-meaning words are used in a limited fashion.	The vocabulary draws on domain-specific, general academic, and multiple-meaning words, with text supports to guide the reader's correct interpretations of their meanings; it represents familiar concepts and ideas.	The vocabulary demand is extensive, domain specific, and representative of complex ideas; little is offered in the way of context clues.

Source: Adapted by Sherrye Dee Garrett, Jeannette Gomez, and Lindsay Bingaman from Fisher, D., Frey, N., & Lapp, D. (2016). *Text complexity*, pp. 72–74. Corwin.

Levels of Meaning and Purpose

This first factor refers to how overtly the text's purpose and meaning are apparent to the reader. Some texts are dense, with lots of ambiguous meanings that can confound a reader's understanding of the text. Poems often draw on density, especially those that rely on literary devices such as allusions to historical or mythological characters and places, such as T. S. Elliot's poem "The Wasteland," which refers to a Phoenician Sailor and the Lady of the Rocks, among others. Informational text can also be dense, especially when lots of nominalizations are used, a common feature of science texts. Nominalizations are verbs and adjectives that have been turned into nouns and are used to describe processes. *Evaporate* is easier to understand than *evaporation*. *Avoid* is easier to understand than *avoidance*.

The true purpose of the text may be intentionally obscured, such as the use of the unreliable narrator in short stories by Edgar Allan Poe. But children's books abound with unreliable narrators. Consider Max in *Where the Wild Things Are* (Sendak, 1963) or the Big Bad Wolf in *The True Story of the Three Little Pigs* (Scieszka 1989). An informational text may present challenges to the purpose, such as an opinion piece that serves as a form of propaganda, or an historical account that presents only one side of an event. Informational texts may also embed the author's viewpoint or value judgments. Keep in mind that the writer's opinion doesn't have to be wrong to be worth interrogating. Even a book on recycling that makes statements about its benefits still suggests the author's viewpoint and is worth discussing with students.

Structure

All texts have an organizational structure, although this easier to discern in some than in others. Most narratives, whether real or imagined, follow a conventional plot-driven story structure:

- *Exposition* (introduction of the theme, setting, characters, and circumstances)
- *Rising action* (the series of events that create interest and tension, and expose the problems and flaws of the characters)

- *Climax* (the emotional high point or peak tension of the story; it addresses the story's biggest question)

- *Falling action* (the events that are a result of the climax)

- *Resolution or denouement* (the final solutions or outcomes of the story)

Young readers initially learn the story grammar of characters, setting, and problem and solution; then they expand to theme, mood, direct and indirect characterization, and so on, throughout elementary and middle school.

Young readers initially learn the story grammar of characters, setting, and problem and solution; then they expand to theme, mood, and direct and indirect characterization.

The more formal language of Freytag's pyramid of dramatic structure (see Figure 5.4) is utilized in high school as a tool for analysis, and while the structure is familiar, the challenge comes in locating the frame within a wider range of texts.

Figure 5.4 Freytag's pyramid.

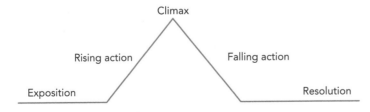

Source: Adapted from Freytag, G. (1863). *Die technik des dramas*. S. Hirzel.

The organizational structure of informational texts differs from that of literary ones, and most use expository structures:

- *Descriptive*: Detailed information about a process, procedure, action, or phenomenon

- *Compare and contrast*: Explanation of similarities and differences

- *Temporal sequence*: Events change or remain the same over time and are explained in a chronological order

- *Cause and effect*: An event is explained in terms of its effect, or the rationale for an effect is explained through its causes

- *Problem and solution*: A problematic situation is presented, and possible, desirable, undesirable, or actual solutions are revealed

Signal words assist readers in detecting these organizational structures. As examples, temporal sequence signal words such as *first, next, last,* and *meanwhile* help students create a mental timeline. Casual connectives such as *so, because,* and *then*; as well as contrastive connectives like *but, not,* and *however*; allow the reader to determine relationships between ideas. Outside of extensively engineered passages for young readers, most informational texts utilize two or more of these expository structures, although one may be dominant. This passage from *The Great Migration*s: *Butterflies* is intended for third-grade science students. Its dominant expository structure is a temporal sequence (underlined), but it contains a contrastive connector (bolded):

> Each year, the monarchs' migration takes several generations. Three or four generations complete the trip north. **But** only one generation makes the return trip south. That means that if you started the journey, your great, great grandchildren would finish it (Marsh, 2010, p. 16).

To further complicate matters, an informational text may include narrative components to enrich the imagery. Writers will often employ a narrative device to enliven informational text and build a bridge to a student's experience. For example, social studies and

> Outside of extensively engineered passages for young readers, most informational texts utilize two or more expository structures, although one may be dominant.

history texts abound with short vignettes about the lives of historical figures and ordinary citizens alike. A passage from a seventh-grade textbook about the medieval period in Europe is likely to include information about the daily life of the children of serfs and the nobility. The presence or absence of such organizational structures contributes to the text's relative complexity.

The text features and graphics included in literary and informational texts lend support to readers. Common text features we rely upon to organize the text include titles, headings, and page numbers. However, other text features assist in locating information (e.g., table of contents), explain and elaborate (e.g., diagrams), illustrate (e.g., photographs), and notify (e.g., italics). A more complete list appears in Figure 5.5. One example is the passage about the migration of monarch butterflies adjacent to a map of North America showing each generation's incremental journey from central Mexico to southern Canada. Some texts will include specific callouts to signal when the reader should consult a text figure, as this text does when it directs your attention to a chart. However, not all do, and this can be a point of confusion for inexperienced readers who have difficulty incorporating additional information into their reading. Contemporary picture books and informational articles for school use often contain an overwhelming number of text features that vie for a reader's attention. Specific instruction on how to consolidate this information is useful for readers who are still learning how to utilize graphical and textual features.

Language Convention and Clarity

A third contributing factor of text complexity is the extent to which the language conventions conform to those already known to the reader. Shakespearean plays and sonnets are complex in part because the Early Modern English vernacular of the time is not one wholly familiar to 21st century readers. Therefore, the archaic language of the time interferes with comprehension, even when the human condition of jealousy, love, and conflict does not.

The clarity of a piece can also confound and is apparent when the original intended audience differs from current readers. Here are two passages to serve as contrasting examples. The first is from developmental psychologist Jean Piaget's work on language and thinking in

Figure 5.5 Common text features and graphic elements and their functions.

Function	Text Features
Elements that organize	• Chapters
	• Titles
	• Headings
	• Subheadings
	• List of figures
Elements for locating information	• Table of contents
	• Indexes
	• Page numbers
Elements for explanation and elaboration	• Diagrams
	• Charts and tables
	• Graphs
	• Glossary
Elements that illustrate	• Photographs
	• Illustrations
Elements that notify	• Bolded words
	• Italics and other changes in font

Source: Fisher, D., Frey, N., & Lapp, D. (2008). *In a reading state of mind: Brain research, teacher modeling, and comprehension instruction.* Newark, DE: International Reading Association.

children; it was written for fellow academics. The second passage is from a high school psychology textbook discussing Piaget's work:

> An adult is at once more highly individualized and far more highly socialized than a child forming part of such a society. He is more individualized, since he can work in private without announcing what he is doing, and without imitating his neighbours. . . . The child is neither individualized, since he cannot keep a single thought secret, and since everything done by one member of the group is repeated through a sort of imitative repercussion by almost every other member, nor is he socialized, since this imitation is not accompanied by what may properly called an interchange of thought, about half the remarks made by children being **ego-centric** in character. (Piaget, 1974, p. 61)

The passage below is from the textbook for Advanced Placement high school students:

> Piaget contended that preschool children are **egocentric**: they have difficulty perceiving things from another's viewpoint. Asked to "show Mommy your picture," 2-year-old Gabriella holds the picture up facing her own eyes. Three-year-old Gray makes himself "invisible," assuming that if he can't see his grandparents, they can't see him. . . . They simply have not yet developed the ability to take another's viewpoint. (Myers, 2009, pp. 478–479)

While both passages discuss a developmental stage Piaget called *egocentric*, the writers' approaches differ in how the stage is explained to the reader. Piaget discusses what adults can do at length and leaves his reader to infer how preschool children behave. The high school textbook passage provides direct examples of young children's thinking. Piaget assumes that his fellow researchers already know what toddlers do, and he doesn't need to provide representations. However, the writer of the textbook knows his readers have no formal experience observing young children, and therefore provides examples that adolescents have probably seen in younger siblings.

Both of these passages highlight the *register* of the language, which describes the relative formality of the language. All of us use a variety of registers when we speak and write, each influenced by the social relationship we have with the listener or reader. Our ability to use the right register is influenced by our ability to detect the sociolinguistic context and properly match it. There are five language registers (Joos, 1967):

- *Fixed or frozen.* Fixed speech is reserved for traditions in which the language does not change. Examples of fixed speech include the Pledge of Allegiance, Shakespeare plays, and civil ceremonies such as weddings.

- *Formal.* At the formal level, speech is expected to be presented in complete sentences with specific word usage. Formal language is the standard for work, school, and business and is more often seen in writing than in speaking. However, public speeches and presentations are expected to be delivered in a formal language register.

- *Consultative.* The third level of language, consultative, is a formal register used in conversations. Less appropriate for writing, students often use consultative language in their interactions in the classroom.

- *Casual.* This is the language that is used in conversation with friends. In casual speech, word choice is general, and conversation is dependent upon nonverbal assists, significant background knowledge, and shared information.

- *Intimate.* This is the language used by very close friends and lovers. Intimate speech is private and often requires a significant amount of shared history, knowledge, and experience.

To return to the previous passages on child development, Piaget's language register is quite formal, while the high school textbook employs a bit more consultative language register. Literary texts often employ multiple registers in dialogue to demonstrate the relationships between characters. For example, the dialogue in *Charlotte's Web* (White, 1952) between Wilbur and Charlotte changes from casual to intimate as their friendship deepens. Fern's mother's language register when she speaks with Dr. Dorian, the family physician, is consultative, as she shares her worry about her daughter's reports of talking with spiders. A reader's familiarity with the register being used can contribute greatly to understanding of the text.

Literacy texts often employ multiple registers in dialogue to demonstrate the relationships between characters. . . . A reader's familiarity with the register being used can contribute greatly to understanding of the text.

Knowledge Demands

A fourth qualitative factor in text complexity is the knowledge demand of the reader. For now, we will limit discussion to the characteristics of the text itself. *Background knowledge* is reflected in experience, while *prior knowledge* is formal and likely acquired in school. Both can be utilized by readers to comprehend text. A literary example is Gwendolyn Brooks's (1963) poem "We Real Cool." In 32 words, Brooks draws heavily on the background knowledge of adolescents who can readily conjure up a picture of young men who dropped out of school, turned to a nefarious life, and will likely "die soon." Although the words are simple to decode, their darker meaning would be lost on elementary students. That same adolescent reader is also drawing on prior knowledge about the poem's form, noting that it has four stanzas, a three-meter beat, and a couplet rhyme scheme that forces a cadence as it is read aloud.

Informational texts may present a challenge for readers when it comes to background knowledge. A life science student isn't going to have lived experience at the microscopic level, but the writer who links algae growth to the green pond scum in an accompanying photograph is both building formal knowledge and linking it to a sight familiar to many children. At times this may be closely related to vocabulary knowledge. That same article about algae will include definitional information and will use the term several times so that middle school readers become more comfortable with use of the word *algae* (a much better term than "pond scum").

Informational texts may present a challenge for readers when it comes to background knowledge.

A final consideration as it relates to knowledge is the cultural context. This can be difficult to discern when cultural references are familiar to you, as there may be a mistaken assumption that these allusions are widely known. Western literature often contains Judeo-Christian references of biblical origin. However, a reference to a series of challenges facing a character as being similar to "the trials of Job" may be lost on a student who doesn't know the Old Testament story of a series of misfortunes that test a man's faith. A character who is called a "doubting Thomas" because he demands physical proof might not be perceived by the reader as being disparaged by his friends because he won't readily agree with them. References to other texts, not just religious ones, can add to a text's complexity.

References to other texts, not just religious ones, can add to a text's complexity.

The Special Case of Digital Texts

New digital technologies have made it much easier to access texts for students. As adults, most of us will admit that we do more digital reading today than we did even five years ago. But what effect, if

iStock.com/FatCamera

What effect, if any, does a digital format have on reading comprehension?

Digital texts

any, does a digital format have on reading comprehension? Are there affordances or hinderances that screen reading places on a reader? We are not talking about overall screen usage across a child's day, but rather the school-based use of digital texts. A number of research studies have examined this question, and while the effects are still in question, some trends are emerging.

The most extensive research to date has been a systematic review of 36 studies from 2001 to 2017 on reading digitally and on paper (Singer & Alexander, 2017). A majority of these studies (75%) were conducted with students in middle school through college. They examined how reading comprehension was defined and assessed in these comparative studies, and they looked for trends. They noted that there was a blurring in these studies between *reading digitally* with the emphasis on the medium, and *digital reading*, with the focus on the navigation and cognitive skills necessary in an online environment. The researchers expressed concern that assessment and student performance is impacted by the digital presentation of the reading. One concerning finding was that across studies, students who had read digitally and then were assessed digitally performed similarly to those in print when it came to basic comprehension questions. However, they did worse than their paper-reading peers when asked more detailed and nuanced questions. Text length of digital readings seemed to negatively impact reading comprehension in these conditions. Students who read digital texts of more than 500 words did not perform as well as those who read less than 500 words. The researchers stated that this should not be "a horse race question" but rather called for future research that more fully explores the differences between the two, such that teachers and assessment designers can better align what is being read with how it is assessed.

The 2019 National Assessment of Educational Progress (NAEP) test scores provide more troubling data. The test, often called "the Nation's report card," assesses a representative sample of fourth- and eighth-grade students in the United States. Using background information garnered from tested students and their teachers, the results of the reading portion of the assessment were compared with the amount of time spent using a digital device daily during language arts instruction. The results showed that at both grade levels, there was an inverse association between higher amounts of digital usage and lower reading test scores (see Figure 5.6).

Figure 5.6 Digital device use during language arts and NAEP 2019 reading scores.

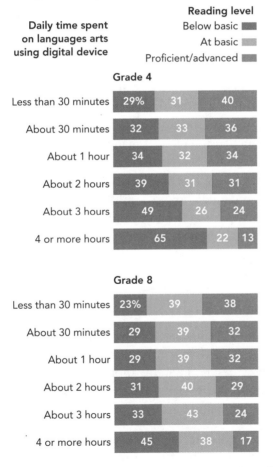

Daily time spent on languages arts using digital device

Reading level
Below basic ▪
At basic ▪
Proficient/advanced ▪

Grade 4

Daily time	Below basic	At basic	Proficient/advanced
Less than 30 minutes	29%	31	40
About 30 minutes	32	33	36
About 1 hour	34	32	34
About 2 hours	39	31	31
About 3 hours	49	26	24
4 or more hours	65	22	13

Grade 8

Daily time	Below basic	At basic	Proficient/advanced
Less than 30 minutes	23%	39	38
About 30 minutes	29	39	32
About 1 hour	29	39	32
About 2 hours	31	40	29
About 3 hours	33	43	24
4 or more hours	45	38	17

Source: Sparks, S.D. (2019). Screen time up as reading scores drop, Is there a link? *Education Week, 39*(13), 1, 12.

Note: Percentages may not add to 100 due to rounding.

Is it the format of the assessment, reading digitally, or a combination of both? Although computers have been available in classrooms for 25 years, it has only been in the last decade that a wide array of digital devices has been used so much, stated Alexander in an interview about the findings. "Here's what we do know about reading: You read better when you read in print, meaning you remember more of what you read, you understand it deeper, . . . We keep trying to understand why, because study after study, this is happening" (Sparks, 2019, p. 12).

> You read better when you read in print, meaning you remember more of what you read, you understand it deeper. . . . We keep trying to understand why, because study after study, this is happening" (Sparks, 2019, p. 12).

Reading teachers in this century face an additional question that was not in play at the turn of this century, and that is whether we should be concerned about the impact of online reading outside of school. First, it is much too early in this phenomenon to fully understand whether there is an impact, positively or negatively, on reading comprehension. There are early studies on the topic that have been done that are correlational in nature, so relationships they reveal should not be misunderstood as causational. That said, the more time spent outside of school reading fragmented digital information typical in emails, chats, and social media postings, the lower the student's reading comprehension of print materials is likely to be (Pfost et al., 2013). Again, it is unclear what the contributing factors might be. Is it that the short length of these texts encourages more rapid attentional shifts and therefore undermines stamina for reading longer texts? The researchers in this study further speculate that the content and quality of digital texts on smartphones and in social media is less robust. Whatever the contributing causes, continued attention to digital and print reading is warranted.

Texts in Primary Grades

We have devoted the first part of this chapter to discussing the complexity of the text. However, texts in primary grades are used for other purposes besides building knowledge and language capabilities. There are specially engineered texts whose express purpose is to build the reading skills of emergent readers.

Consider the dilemma facing kindergarten teacher Kendall Donovan. Most of her students are at the earliest phase of emergent reading. They are learning letter names and sounds, can recognize their names, and possess a growing bank of common words and sight words. She has several students who are a bit more advanced, and Ms. Donovan is regularly moving them forward through leveled books that are challenging their reading skills. In addition, she has a precocious reader in the form of Ewell, who arrived on the first day of school already reading early chapter books.

But Ms. Donovan knows that her students need access to a span of books that perform different functions. There are four types in particular that are essential for her:

- *Decodable texts* that are phonetically regular and designed to build sound/letter correspondence. These are engineered to keep the less decodable words to a minimum while repeating specific patterns to reinforce decoding skills. The sentences are short and have limited meaning-making opportunities. A highly decodable text has sentences like this: "Pam sees a ram. The ram sees Pam. Pam and the ram ran!"

- *Controlled-vocabulary texts* are constructed to reduce the number of rare words as measured by grade-level lists. New words are introduced systematically and used frequently to create more practice opportunities. Unlike decodable texts, there are more sight words included, and comprehension instruction is more feasible. Dr. Seuss's *One Fish Two Fish Red Fish Blue Fish* (1960) is a glorious example of a controlled vocabulary text.

- *Predictable-pattern texts* are used by the teacher to further build sound/word associations through repetition. Books like *The Napping House* (Wood, 1984) tell a cumulative story that allows her students to have repeated practice with a growing chant: *"And on that granny / there is a child / a dreaming child / on a snoring granny / on a cozy bed / in a napping house, / where everyone is sleeping."* They are soon joined by a snoozing cat, a dozing dog, and so on.

- *Authentic texts* are those written for young audiences, although not necessarily for reading instruction. They are primarily read to and with children and extend their listening comprehension. A book such as *A Bike Like Sergio's*

(Boelts, 2016) provides rich discussion about ethical dilemmas and responsibility. However, books such as these are not useful for reading instruction in primary grades, as there are too many rare words and little opportunity to practice.

Ms. Donovan makes strategic decisions about the types of texts she utilizes such that they maximize learning opportunities. For instance, during her small group teacher-directed instruction, Ms. Donovan uses decodable and controlled-vocabulary texts to develop her students' emergent reading skills.

"I use these texts to align with the systematic phonics curriculum we use in the district," she explained. "That way I'm making sure there aren't gaps along the way."

But Ms. Donovan uses predictable-pattern texts and authentic literature to promote language acquisition and to develop knowledge. "These aren't books my kids are going to be able to read independently, and if they could, the texts wouldn't be complex enough anyway," she said. "My intention is to build their listening comprehension and their knowledge, because that contributes to their reading development," she said.

Making decisions
about texts

Making Decisions About Text

A decision-making process is essential in reading comprehension instruction, as Ms. Donovan shared. It is not sufficient to simply rely upon a reading program to do the selecting for you. Reading programs are designed with a broad array of teachers and students in mind and do their best to provide educators with a plethora of material. But it is up to skilled educators to make choices that are intentional and that serve students well. The text does not stand alone, nor does the student or the task. All three elements interact with one another in myriad ways. Yet among the three, the characteristics of the students are in the least control of the teacher. These characteristics include their cognitive capabilities, knowledge, motivation, and experiences. Note that we didn't say "no control." In fact, we can influence students' knowledge, motivation, and experiences. Collectively, those speak to the skill, will, and thrill of comprehension that is the overarching theme of this book, and each is described in detail in a previous chapter. Having said that, the choice of text and associated tasks are completely under the control of the teacher (Valencia et al., 2014). We suggest a model for text selection that incorporates considerations of the text and the student(s), as well as the task. Task consideration, whether it is teacher led, peer led, or independent, is the focus of the remaining part of this chapter.

Tasks as Tools for Fostering Comprehension

The nature of the text is a crucial consideration, but there is more to learning to read. Simply having students do lots of reading without accompanying instruction is not going to yield consistent results. We pair texts with tasks in order to construct learning events that foster our students' reading comprehension. By *tasks,* we don't mean student work production. There are lots of student work examples, such as writing an informational report, speaking extemporaneously about a topic, or completing an exit slip at the end of class. Rather, we think of tasks through the lens of cognitive and metacognitive demands. In other words, what kinds of thinking are needed? In what ways are students required to think about their thinking? In order to create conditions for cognition and metacognition, teachers utilize two instructional tools—direct instruction and dialogic instruction—so that students learn.

> We think of tasks through the lens of cognitive and metacognitive demands. In other words, what kinds of thinking are needed? In what ways are students required to think about their thinking?

Direct and Dialogic Instruction

Learning is social, a lesson that Vygotsky (1978) taught us. We learn by closely observing others and mimicking what they do. In fact, our brains are hardwired to do this, through a network of specialized cells called mirror neurons (Iacoboni et al., 2005). The ability to mimic is critical for survival of the species as we learn what is dangerous and what will keep us safe. We also learn by trading information with others. Our species's ability to use spoken language to convey information to others and gain knowledge in return resulted in an explosion of advancement among humans. As teachers we use these same ancient mechanisms to teach. That mirror neuron system in our students' brains makes it possible for us to provide direct instruction of new skills and strategies such that they can begin to imitate cognitive and metacognitive actions. This new knowledge is further refined and deepened through teacher-led and peer-led

Dialogic instruction includes generating questions, engaging in discussion, and listening carefully to the ideas of others.

dialogic instruction. Dialogic instruction includes generating questions, engaging in discussion, and listening carefully to the ideas of others. Together, direct and dialogic instruction constitute the ways we create cognitive and metacognitive learning tasks.

Direct Instruction

There is arguably no more misunderstood instructional tool than direct instruction. Some educators perceive that direct instruction is didactic and scripted and that it does not allow for teacher judgment. However, this isn't the case. Direct instruction is a form of instructional guidance that is structured, sequenced, and teacher led (Kirschner et al., 2006). Sometimes called "small d.i." to distinguish it from a commercial product of the same name, the researchers refer to direct instructional guidance as "providing information that fully explains the concepts and procedures that students are required to learn as well as learning strategy support that is compatible with human cognitive architecture" (p. 75). Direct instruction is in evidence when teachers do any of the following (Fisher et al., 2016):

- Establish learning intentions and success criteria for students to set the stage for learning

- Model expert thinking and demonstrate skills and concepts

- Check for understanding throughout a lesson in order to make adjustments

- Provide guided instruction such that learners can practice new skills and concepts with feedback from the teacher

- Close a lesson with a summary to organize student thinking and consolidate learning

Direct instruction

Sixth-grade teacher Luz Salcedo uses direct instruction in virtually every lesson. If she is teaching a new skill or concept, a larger proportion of the lesson is dedicated to direct instruction; when her students are deepening their knowledge through dialogic avenues, fewer minutes of direct instruction are needed. During a small group close reading lesson using the prologue of *The Book Thief* (Zusak, 2005), Ms. Salcedo discusses her learning intentions with the four students ("to determine the narrator of this passage"). "This is the introduction to the book," she explains, "and the author uses a unique literary device to tell the story." She begins her direct instruction by thinking aloud about the title: "'Death and Chocolate'. There's something scary and something sweet in that title. I'm already thinking this is going to be about contrasts." She brings their attention to the differences in typeface throughout, as some sentences are set off by asterisks and in bolded capital letters. She reads the prologue aloud while her students follow in their books, pausing occasionally to think aloud about the questions she is generating in her mind. At the end of the passage, she repeats the last line: "I saw the book thief three times" (p. 5).

Using questions, prompts, and cues, she now guides their thinking about possible conclusions. "What's that all about? What does the narrator mean?"

The students skim and scan the passage, and soon Rodrigo and Tessa notice that the unusual typeface has also occurred three times.

"What if you read just those three sections?" asks the teacher. Jillian volunteers to read them aloud. "What are your thoughts?" Ms. Salcedo asks. "Do they go together, or not?" Ms. Salcedo's instruction is now moving into dialogic discussion, so we will continue the lesson in the next section.

Dialogic Instruction

When we create space for students to generate questions, wrestle with complex issues, clarify thinking, speculate, probe, disagree, resolve problems, and reach consensus, we are engaging in dialogic instruction. These acts form the heart of discussion. Through discussion with classmates and the teacher, students deepen their understanding as they co-construct knowledge and broaden their schema. Classroom discussion, it should be noted, is defined as communication between at least three people for at least 30 seconds. In practice, however, it is quite rare. One review of the research on the topic found that discussion in middle and high school English classrooms averaged between 14 and 68 *seconds* per class period (Wilkinson & Nelson, 2013). More typical is the teacher-led interaction Cazden (1998) described as initiate-respond-evaluate (IRE). Notice that the

> Classroom discussion, it should be noted, is defined as communication between at least three people for at least 30 seconds. In practice, however, it is quite rare.

teacher remains in control of the discussion, often asking low-level recall questions:

> **Teacher:** What is the difference between a simile and a metaphor? [Initiate]
>
> **Student:** A simile uses *as* or *like,* and a metaphor doesn't. [Respond]
>
> **Teacher:** Exactly. [Evaluate]

We all use IRE as a questioning pattern—it is human nature to ask and answer questions. But an exchange like this isn't dialogic. In fact, a different set of skills is needed by the teacher in order to create opportunities to deepen students' cognitive and metacognitive thinking. These conversational moves open up the discussion to allow for students to do the thinking (Michaels et al., 2010). These dialogic teaching methods are part of the larger work of accountable talk, an approach pioneered by the University of Pittsburgh's Institute for Learning. However, more attention has been given to the student-facing side of accountable talk, especially in the use of language frames to support student-directed discussion. These are quite useful, but unless the teacher is modeling how discussion becomes a true exchange, student accountable talk is hindered. The conversational moves of the teacher, outlined in Figure 5.7, provide students with a model as well as the space to engage in critical thinking.

Dialogic instruction

Sixth-grade teacher Luz Salcedo's small group close reading of the prologue of *The Book Thief* is moving from direct to more dialogic instruction. She has just posed a question about three interspersed short passages.

"Do they go together, or not?" she asks.

Khalia, a student in the group, replies, "Well, maybe, but I'm not sure. Like, I think the author is doing something with the font, 'cause it's all the same. But I don't know what it means."

Ms. Salcedo replies, "So you're saying it seems like it must be connected. But you don't know how. Who agrees or disagrees?" she asks the others.

Figure 5.7 Teacher moves to foster accountable talk.

Conversational Move	Example
Marking conversation	"That's an important point."
Keeping the channels open	"Did everyone hear what she just said?"
Keeping everyone together	"Who can repeat . . . ?"
Challenging students	"That's a great question, Rebecca. What do others think?"
Revoicing	"So you're saying that. . . ."
Asking students to explain or restate	"Who disagrees or agrees, and why?"
Linking contributions	"Who can add on to what he said?"
Pressing for accuracy	"Where can we find that?"
Building on prior knowledge	"How does this connect with . . . ?"
Pressing for reasoning	"Why do you think that?"
Expanding reasoning	"Take your time. Say more."
Recapping	"What have we discovered?"

Source: Michaels, S., O'Connor, M. C., Hall, M. W., & Resnick, L. B. (2010). *Accountable Talk® Sourcebook: For Classroom Conversation That Works* (v.3.1). University of Pittsburgh Institute for Learning. Retrieved from http://ifl.lrdc.pitt.edu

Now Rodrigo adds, "I agree that they go together, but there's this stuff in there about colors and I don't get it."

"Say more about that. Can you turn it into a question?" the teacher asks.

After pausing, the boy says, "I don't know who the 'I' is. I don't know who's talking."

The teacher smiles. "That's a great question. Did everyone hear that? Who is the narrator? That's going to be really important in the story, right?" She looks at all of them and says, "You've got a bit of reading to do. You've got the question that Rodrigo asked: Who is the narrator? Read the next five pages to complete the prologue, and I'll check in with you tomorrow. Once we've got that figured out, your book club will be off and running."

Direct instruction and dialogic instruction form two major components teachers use to foster learning. The cognitive and metacognitive tasks students undertake are the result of these approaches. We have further expanded these approaches across an instructional framework—the gradual release of responsibility. The intent of the framework is to embed these approaches into a set of instructional moves that ensure learning occurs.

An Instructional Framework That Works

Our experience suggests that a classroom structured on a gradual release of responsibility model will ensure that students are apprenticed with intention in order to develop their expertise. This model moves readers across the divide as they assume more of the cognitive load for applying the strategies. Consistent with the movement from apprentice to expert, as well as with Vygotsky's concept of movement between zones of proximal development, the gradual release of responsibility instructional framework acknowledges the role of the teacher in guiding students to independent practice or application (Fisher & Frey, 2007; Pearson & Gallagher, 1983). Our work on the gradual release of responsibility model centers on four instructional routines. Importantly, the structure is not linear but rather is recursive, meaning that each of the routines is used flexibly in the classroom. Let's briefly consider each of the four routines (see Figure 5.8).

An instructional framework that works

Figure 5.8 A framework for gradual release of responsibility.

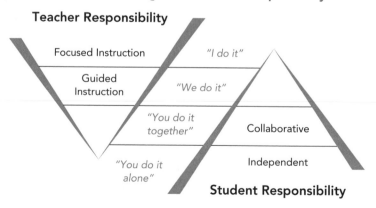

Source: Fisher, D., & Frey, N. (2014). *Better learning through structured teaching: A framework for the gradual release of responsibility* (2nd ed.), p. 3. ASCD.

Focused Instruction

Typically delivered to the whole class, focus lessons are usually 15 minutes or less in length. The focus lesson contains two parts. First, the teacher establishes the purpose of the lesson by setting forth learning intentions and success criteria. Establishing purpose has been shown to be a critical component of instruction, especially for English language learners who often are unsure which parts of the class to pay attention to (Hill & Flynn, 2006). Learning intentions, which establish purpose, can be established in a number of domains, such as content, language, and social learning. For example, one teacher might suggest a focus on "using literary devices to understand themes from literature," while another might focus on "specific words authors use to make their case or to persuade the reader." The content purpose should align with standards but not simply be the standards read aloud. Rather, daily learning intentions are incremental steps toward mastery of the standards. Teachers who consistently ensure that their students reach high levels of proficiency establish content and language purposes daily.

The second component of focus instruction is modeling thinking, which is critical for students as they are provided with examples of the use of strategies that they can incorporate on their own. As noted earlier, direct instruction is a strong feature in this phase of learning.

Guided Instruction

The second routine, guided instruction, involves the teacher guiding students through tasks. This is typically accomplished with small, purposefully selected groups of students. These groups are created based on formative assessment information and thus are changed regularly. In meeting with small groups of students, the teacher can provide additional prompts, cues, and questions to get the students to do the thinking. The key to effective guided instruction is the link between small group instruction and the focus lesson. For example, if the purpose were to identify words that persuaded a reader, students might be asked to write a persuasive paragraph. These paragraphs may then be used as fodder for a guided instruction session in which the teacher asks questions of students about the persuasive nature of the selections. In addition, the teacher must remember that the guided instruction should transfer more responsibility for thinking

> The key to effective guided instruction is the link between small group instruction and the focus lesson.

to the students. Guided instruction forwards the move to teacher-led dialogic instruction, as students are assuming more of the cognitive and metacognitive load.

Collaborative Learning

When students work together in small groups, they use peer-led dialogic learning to consolidate their thinking. These collaborative learning groups might meet while the teacher is working with needs-based groups in guided instruction, or in parallel with other collaborative groups. Again, the tasks of the collaborative learning group must be aligned with the focused instruction and allow students, with their peers, to apply what they are learning. In this way, students talk with one another about the skills and strategies they use as they read, and they can assist one another in making decisions about what to do when stuck. For example, during a lesson on persuasion, students might read selections in pairs or triads and discuss the ways in which the author used words to attempt to persuade readers.

Social learning theory tells us that humans learn from the interactions they have with others. As Bandura (1977) noted, "Learning would be exceedingly laborious, not to mention hazardous, if people had to rely solely on the effects of their own actions to inform them what to do" (p. 22). Through peer support, students assume greater cognitive and metacognitive responsibility for their comprehension, and they receive feedback from others about the strategies they use. In this way, the strategies begin to become skills and not simply something that the teacher talks about.

Through peer support, students assume greater cognitive and metacognitive responsibility for their comprehension, and they receive feedback from others about the strategies they use.

Independent Learning

The final routine is independent learning—the goal of schooling. Unfortunately, too many students are assigned independent learning tasks for which they have not yet received adequate instruction to be successful. The gradual release of responsibility instructional framework requires that learners have multiple opportunities to engage with facts, concepts, and literacy strategies before they're expected to use them on their own. In fact, we would go so far as to say that without this level of instruction support, students will experience a "failure to launch." Instead of ensuring that students become skilled readers who apply what they know automatically and unconsciously, and who can slow down and purposefully apply strategies to challenging texts, we risk creating readers who have a definitional knowledge of reading strategies yet who fail to use them in real time and with real texts. Students in the independent phase of learning are marshalling their skills in order to make meaning from text, and utilizing problem-solving strategies when meaning breaks down. In order to do so, students need frequent opportunities to apply what they have learned using texts that stretch their thinking just a bit more than it was stretched last week.

Conclusion

Texts and accompanying instruction compose two powerful tools in the reading comprehension toolkit. In turn, each demands careful decision making in order to tailor learning to meet the needs of students. Analysis of texts has advanced considerably, and quantitative measures are easily accessible to teachers and curriculum leaders. Quantitative tools must be balanced with qualitative measures that provide the dimensionality we need to make wise selections. The overall benefit to us as educators is that the knowledge that comes with the use of these tools provides knowledge of what we are teaching, and how we might anticipate the challenges in order to teach with precision.

The instruction that accompanies robust texts further influences student learning. Careful alignment between what the text offers and the amount of instruction needed can accelerate student learning. However, this cannot occur when recitational lessons abound, with little opportunity for students to assume more of the cognitive responsibility. But when thoughtful educators consider the text and task as dynamic variables, students face the potential of significant gains in reading comprehension. We do not believe in a laissez-faire approach to learning. We don't believe that learning occurs just because you fill a room with books, put beanbags and pillows in the corners, and then give kids unstructured reading time. Teach with a sense of urgency. Teach with intention. Your students will thank you for it.

Teach with a sense of urgency. Teach with intention. Your students will thank you for it.

References

Adams, M. J. (1990). *Beginning to read: Thinking and learning about print.* MIT Press.

Afflerbach, P., Pearson, P. D., & Paris, S. (2008). Clarifying differences between reading skills and reading strategies. *The Reading Teacher, 61*(5), 364–373.

Alcott, L. M. (2006). *Little women.* First World Library.

Alexander, P. A., & Jetton, T. L. (2000). Learning from text: A multidimensional and developmental perspective. In M. L. Kamil, P. B. Mosenthal, P. D. Pearson, & R. Barr (Eds.), *Handbook of reading research* (vol. III, pp. 285–310). Erlbaum.

Alexander, K. (2015). *The crossover.* HMH Books for Young Readers.

Anderson, P., Wilson, P., & Fielding, L. (1988). Growth in reading and how children spend their time outside of school. *Reading Research Quarterly, 23*(3), 285–303.

Anderson, R. C. (2013). Role of reader's schema in comprehension, learning, and memory. In D. E. Alvermann, N. J. Unrau, & R. B. Ruddell (Eds.), *Theoretical models and processes of reading* (6th ed, pp. 476–488). International Reading Association.

Anderson, R. C., & Pearson, P. D. (1984). A schema-theoretic view of basic processes in reading comprehension. In P. D. Pearson (Ed.), *Handbook of reading research* (vol. 1, pp. 255–291). Longman.

Araújo, S., Reis, A., Petersson, K. J., & Faísca, L. (2015). Rapid automatized naming and reading performance: A meta-analysis. *Journal of Educational Psychology, 107*(3), 868–883.

Aronson, E., Bridgeman, D., & Geffner, R. (1978). Interdependent interactions and prosocial behavior. *Journal of Research and Development in Education, 12*(1), 16–27.

Ausubel, D. (1968). *Educational psychology: A cognitive view.* Holt, Rinehart, & Winston.

Baker, S. K., Smolkowski, K., Katz, R., Fien, H., Seeley, J. R., Kame'enui, E. J., & Beck, C. T. (2008). Reading fluency as a predictor of reading proficiency in low-performing high poverty schools. *School Psychology Review, 37*(1), 18–37.

Bakhtin, M. M. (1981). *The dialogic imagination: Four essays* (C. Emerson, Trans.). University of Texas Press.

Bandura, A. (1977). *Social learning theory*. General Learning Press.

Baron, D. (2007). Using text-based protocols: Rendering the text. *Principal Leadership: High School Edition, 7*(7), 46–49.

Baumann, J. F., Kame'enui, E. J., & Ash, G. E. (2003). Research on vocabulary instruction: Voltaire redux. In J. Flood, D. Lapp, J. R. Squire, & J. M. Jensen (Eds.), *Handbook on teaching the English language arts* (2nd ed., pp. 752–785). Erlbaum.

Beck, I. L., McKeown, M. G., & Kucan, L. (2013). *Bringing words to life: Robust vocabulary instruction* (2nd ed.). Guilford.

Beck, I. L., McKeown, M. G., Sandora, C., Kucan, L., & Worthy, J. (1996). Questioning the author. *The Elementary School Journal, 96*(4), 395–414.

Becker, M., McElvany, N., & Kortenbruck, M. (2010). Intrinsic and extrinsic reading motivation as predictors of reading literacy: A longitudinal study. *Journal of Educational Psychology, 102*(4), 773–785.

Bishop, R. S. (1990). Mirrors, windows, and sliding glass doors. *Perspectives, 1*(3), ix–xi.

Block, C. C., & Lacina, J. (2009). Comprehension instruction in kindergarten through grade three. In S. E. Israel & G. G. Duffy (Eds.), *Handbook of research on reading comprehension* (pp. 494–509). Routledge.

Bloom, B. (1986). Automaticity: The hands and feet of genius. *Educational Leadership, 43*(5), 70-77.

Boelts, M. (2016). *A bike like Sergio's*. New York: Penguin Random House.

Bransford, J. D., Brown, A. L., & Cocking, R. R. (Eds.). (2000). *How people learn: Brain, mind, experience, and school.* Committee on Developments in the Science of Learning and Committee on Learning Research and Educational Practice. National Academy Press.

Bransford, J. D., & Johnson, M. K. (1972). Contextual prerequisites for understanding: Some investigations of comprehension and recall. *Journal of Verbal Learning and Verbal Behavior, 11*(6), 717–726.

Brashares, A. (2001). *Sisterhood of the traveling pants*. Delacorte.

Brookhart, S. M. (2013). Assessing creativity. *Educational Leadership, 70*(5), 28–34.

Brooks, B. (2018). *Stories for boys who dare to be different: True tales of amazing boys who changed the world without killing dragons*. Hatchette.

Brooks, G. (1963). *Selected poems*. HarperCollins.

Brown, A. L. (1987). Metacognition, executive control, self-regulation, and other more mysterious mechanisms. In F. Weinert & R. Kluwe (Eds.), *Metacognition, motivation and understanding* (pp. 393–451). Erlbaum.

Brown, D. (2003). The Da Vinci code. Delacorte Press.

Canales, V. (2005). *The tequila worm.* Random House.

Carney, E. (2012). *Planets.* National Geographic Children's Books.

Cazden, C. B. (1998). *Classroom discourse: The language of teaching and learning.* Heinemann.

Chall, J. (1983). *Stages of reading development.* McGraw-Hill.

Chapman, J. W., & Tunmer, W. E. (2003). Reading difficulties, reading-related self-perceptions, and strategies for overcoming negative self-beliefs. *Reading and Writing Quarterly, 19*(1), 5–24.

Cheng, A. (2015). *When the bees fly home.* Tilbury House Nature Books.

Cheng, L. (1991). *Assessing Asian language performance: Guidelines for evaluating limited-English proficient students* (2nd ed.). Academic Communication Associates.

Chyl, K., Kossowski, B., Dębska, A., Łuniewska, M., Banaszkiewicz, A., Żelechowska, A., Frost, S. J., Mencl, W. E., Wypych, M., Marchewka, A., Pugh, K. R., & Jednoróg, K. (2018). Prereader to beginning reader: Changes induced by reading acquisition in print and speech brain networks. *Journal of Child Psychology & Psychiatry, 59*(1), 76–87.

Cirino, P. T., Miciak, J., Ahmed, Y., Barnes, M. A., Taylor, W. P., & Gerst, E. H. (2019). Executive function: Association with multiple reading skills. *Reading and Writing, 32*(7), 1819–1846.

Clark, A. M., Anderson, R. C., Kuo, L., Kim, I. H., Archodidou, A., & Nguyen-Jahiel, K. (2003). Collaborative reasoning: Expanding ways for children to talk and think in school. *Educational Psychology Review, 15*(2), 181–198.

Claxton, G. (2017). *The learning power approach: Teaching learners to teach themselves.* Corwin.

Claxton, G. (2018). Deep rivers of learning. *Phi Delta Kappan, 99*(6), 45–48.

Clements, A. (2001). *The janitor's boy.* Aladdin.

Coates, T-N. (2015). *Between the world and me.* Random House.

Cooperative Children's Book Center. (n.d.). *Publishing statistics on children's/YA books about people of color and First/Native Nations and by people of color and First/Native Nations authors and illustrators.* Retrieved May 25, 2020, from http://ccbc.education.wisc.edu/books/pcstats.asp

Csikszentmihalyi, M. (2008). *Flow: The psychology of optimal experience.* Harper.

Daane, M. C., Campbell, J. R., Grigg, W. S., Goodman, M. J., and Oranje, A. (2005). *Fourth-grade students reading aloud: NAEP 2002 special study of oral reading* (NCES 2006-469). U.S. Department of Education. Institute of Education Sciences, National Center for Education Statistics.

Daywalt, D. (2013). *The day the crayons quit.* New York: Philomel Books.

Dehaene, S., Cohen, L., Morais, J., & Kolinsky, R. (2015). Illiterate to literate: Behavioural and cerebral changes induced by reading acquisition. *Nature Reviews Neuroscience, 16*(4), 234–244.

Dr. Seuss. (1957). *How the Grinch stole Christmas!* Random House.

Dr. Seuss. (1960). *One fish two fish red fish blue fish.* Random House.

Duffy, G. G. (2002). Foreword. In C. C. Block, L. B. Gambrell, & M. Pressley (Eds.), *Improving comprehension instruction: Rethinking theory and classroom practice* (pp. xiii–xiv). Jossey-Bass.

Durkin, D. (1978). What classroom observations reveals about reading comprehension instruction. *Reading Research Quarterly, 14*(4), 481–533.

Eeds, M., & Wells, D. (1989). Grand conversations: An exploration of meaning construction in literature study groups. *Research in the teaching of English, 23*(1), 4–29.

Eisner, W. (2000). *New York, NY: The big city.* DC Comics.

Estes, E. (2004). *The hundred dresses.* Harcourt.

Filkins, S. (2012). *Socratic seminars. Differentiating instruction strategy guides.* http://www.readwritethink.org/professional-development/strategy-guides/socratic-seminars-30600.html?tab=2#tabs

Fisher, D., & Frey, N. (2007). Implementing a schoolwide literacy framework: Improving achievement in an urban elementary school. *The Reading Teacher, 61*(1), 32–43.

Fisher, D., Frey, N., & Hattie, J. (2016). *Visible learning for literacy.* Corwin.

Fisher, D., Frey, N., & Akhavan, N. (2020). *This is balanced literacy grades K-6,* p. 47. Corwin.

Fitzpatrick, J. (1997). *Phonemic awareness: Playing with sounds to strengthen beginning reading skills.* Creative Teaching Press.

Flavell, J. H. (1979). Metacognition and cognitive monitoring. A new area of cognitive-development inquiry. *American Psychologist, 34*(10), 906–911.

Fox, M. (1998). *Tough Boris.* Voyager.

Frank, A. (1993). *Anne Frank: The diary of a young girl.* Bantam.

Frey, N., & Fisher, D. (2009). *Learning words inside and out: Vocabulary instruction that boosts achievement in all subject areas.* Heinemann.

Frey, N., Fisher, D., & Moore, K. (2009). Literacy letters: Comparative literature and formative assessment. *The ALAN Review, 36*(2), 27–33.

Freytag, G. (1863). *Die technik des dramas.* S. Hirzel.

Galloway, A. M. (2003). *Improving reading comprehension through metacognitive strategy instruction: Evaluating the evidence for the effectiveness of the reciprocal teaching procedure* (Publication No. AAI3092542) [Doctoral dissertation, University of Nebraska–Lincoln]. ProQuest Dissertations and Theses.

Gambrell, L., Palmer, B., Codling, R., & Mazzoni, S. (1996). *Motivation to read profile (MRP)*. National Reading Research Center.

Gardiner, J. R. (1980). *Stone fox*. HarperTrophy.

Golding, W. (1954). *Lord of the flies*. Coward-McCann.

Gottardo, A., Mirza, A., Koh, P. W., Ferreira, A., & Javier, C. (2018). Unpacking listening comprehension: The role of vocabulary, morphological awareness, and syntactic knowledge in reading comprehension. *Reading & Writing*, *31*(8), 1741–1764.

Gough, P., & Tunmer, W. (1986). Decoding, reading, and reading disability. *Remedial and Special Education*, *7*(1), 6–10.

Graves, M. F., & Slater, W. H. (1996). Vocabulary instruction in content areas. In D. Lapp, J. Flood, & N. Farnan (Eds.), *Content area reading and learning: Instructional strategies* (2nd ed., pp. 261–275). Allyn & Bacon.

Grimes, N. (2002). *Bronx masquerade*. Speak.

Guthrie, J. T., Hoa, A. L. W., Wigfield, A., Tonks, S. M., Humenick, N. M., & Littles, E. (2007). Reading motivation and reading comprehension growth in the later elementary years. *Contemporary Educational Psychology*, *32*(3), 282–313.

Hasbrouck, J., & Tindal, G. (2017). *An update to compiled ORF norms* (Technical report no. 1702). Behavioral Research and Teaching, University of Oregon. https://files.eric.ed.gov/fulltext/ED594994.pdf

Hattie Ranking: 252 influences and effect sizes related to student achievement. (n.d.). Retrieved May 25, 2020, from https://visible-learning.org/hattie-ranking-influences-effect-sizes-learning-achievement

Hattie, J., & Donoghue, G. M. (2016). Learning strategies: A synthesis and conceptual model. *Science of Learning*, *1*,16013.https://doi:10.1038/npjscilearn2016

Herber, H. (1978). *Teaching Reading in Content Areas* (2nd ed.). Pearson.

Hill, J., & Flynn, K. (2006). *Classroom instruction that works with English language learners*. ASCD.

Howe, J. (2003). *Horace and Boris but mostly Delores*. Aladdin.

Huang, J., & Chen, G. (2019). From reading strategy instruction to student reading achievement: The mediating role of student motivational factors. *Psychology in the Schools*, *56*(5), 724–740.

Hunt, L. M. (2015). *Fish in a tree*. Penguin.

Hutchins, P. (1986). *The doorbell rang*. Greenwillow.

Hutton, W. (1981). *The nose tree*. Atheneum.

Iacoboni, M., Molnar-Szakacs, I., Gallese, V., Buccino, G., Mazziotta, J. C., & Rizzolatti, G. (2005). Grasping the intentions of others with one's own mirror neuron system. *PLoS Biology*, *3*(3), e79.

Israel, S. (Ed.). (2017). *Handbook of research on reading comprehension* (2nd ed.). Guilford.

Janks, H. (2019). Critical literacy and the importance of reading with and against a text. *Journal of Adolescent & Adult Literacy, 62*(5), 561–564. http://doi:10.1002/jaal.941

Joos, G. (1986). *Theoretical physics* (3rd ed.). Dover.

Joos, M. (1967). *Five clocks*. Harcourt.

King, A. (1992). Facilitating elaborative learning through guided student-generated questioning. *Educational Psychologist, 27*(11), 111–126.

Kirschner, P. A., Sweller, J., & Clark, R. E. (2006) Why minimal guidance during instruction does not work: An analysis of the failure of constructivist, discovery, problem-based, experiential, and inquiry-based teaching. *Educational Psychologist, 41*(2), 75–86.

LaBerge, D., & Samuels, S. (1974). Toward a theory of automatic information processing in reading. *Cognitive Psychology, 6*(2), 293–332.

Lahiri, J. (2004). *The namesake*. Houghton-Mifflin Harcourt.

Lamott, A. (1995). *Bird by bird: Some instructions on writing and life*. Anchor.

Larson, K. (2006). *Hattie big sky*. Delacorte.

MacGillivray, L., & Martinez, A. M. (1998). Princesses who commit suicide: Primary children writing within and against gender stereotyping. *Journal of Literacy Research, 30*(1), 53–84.

Manyak, P. C., Von Gunten, H., Autenrieth, D., Gillis, C., Mastre-O'Farrell, J., Irvine-McDermott, E., Baumann, J. F., & Blachowicz, L. Z. (2014). Four practical principles for enhancing vocabulary instruction. *The Reading Teacher, 68*(1), 13–23.

Marsh, L. (2010). *Great migrations: Butterflies*. Penguin Random House.

Martinez, M., Roser, N., & Strecker, S. (1998). "I never thought I could be a star": A readers theatre ticket to fluency. *Reading Teacher, 52*(4), 326–334.

Mashburn, A. J., Justice, L. M., Downer, J. T., & Pianta, R. C. (2009). Peer effects on children's language achievement during pre-kindergarten. *Child Development, 80*(3), 686–702.

McCloud, S. (1994). *Understanding comics: The invisible art*. Harper.

McKeown, R. G., & Gentilucci, J. L. (2007). Think-aloud strategy: Metacognitive development and monitoring comprehension in the middle school second-language classroom. *Journal of Adolescent & Adult Literacy, 51*(2), 136–147.

McLaughlin, M., & DeVoogd, G. L. (2004). *Critical literacy: Enhancing students' comprehension of text*. Scholastic.

McNamara, D. S., & Kintsch, W. (1996). Learning from texts: Effects of prior knowledge and text coherence. *Discourse Processes, 22*(3), 247–282.

Mcquillan, J., & Conde, G. (1996). The conditions of flow in reading: Two studies of optimal experience. *Reading Psychology, 17*(2), 109–135.

Mello, R. (2001). Cinderella meets Ulysses. *Language Arts, 78*(6), 548–555.

Michaels, S., O'Connor, M. C., Hall, M. W., & Resnick, L. B. (2010). *Accountable talk® sourcebook: For classroom conversation that works* (v.3.1). University of Pittsburgh Institute for Learning. http://ifl.lrdc.pitt .edu

Millis, K., Magliano, J., Wiemer-Hastings, K., Todaro, S., & McNamara, D. S. (2013). Assessing and improving comprehension with latent semantic analysis. In T. K. Landauer, D. S. McNamara, S. Dennis, & W. Kintsch (Eds.), *Handbook of latent semantic analysis* (pp. 207–226). Lawrence Erlbaum Associates.

Muhammad, G. (2019). Protest, power, and possibilities: The need for agitation literacies. *Journal of Adolescent & Adult Literacy, 63*(3), 351–355.

Murphy, P. K., Wilkinson, I. A. G., Soter, A. O., Hennessey, M. N., & Alexander, J. F. (2009). Examining the effects of classroom discussion on students' comprehension of text: A meta-analysis. *Journal of Educational Psychology, 101*(3), 740–764.

Myers, D. G. (2009). *Psychology in modules* (9th ed.). Worth.

Nagy, W. E., & Anderson, R. C. (1984). How many words are in printed school English? *Reading Research Quarterly, 19*(3), 304–330.

National Reading Panel. (2000). *Teaching children to read: An evidence-based assessment of the scientific research literature on reading and its implications for reading instruction. Reports of the subgroups.* (NIH publication no. 00–4769). National Institute of Child Health and Human Development.

Neuman, S. B., Copple, C., & Bredekamp, S. (2000). *Learning to read and write: Developmentally appropriate practices for young children.* National Association for the Education of Young Children.

Nichols, W. D., Rupley, W. H., & Rasinski, T. (2009). Fluency in learning to read for meaning: Going beyond repeated readings. *Literacy Research & Instruction, 48*(1), 1–13.

Oczkus, L. (2004). *Super six reading strategies: 35 lessons and more for reading success.* Christopher Gordon.

Orwell, G. (1949/2017). *Nineteen eighty-four: A novel.* Houghton-Mifflin Harcourt.

Palincsar, A. S., & Brown, A. L. (1984). Reciprocal teaching of comprehension-fostering and comprehension-monitoring activities. *Cognition and Instruction, 1*(2), 117–175.

Palincsar, A. S., Marcum, M. B., Fitzgerald, M., & Sherwood, C. A. (2019). Braiding teacher practice and class-wide dialogue: An historical inquiry across three sociocultural interventions. *International Journal of Educational Research, 97*(1), 157–165.

Paris, S. G. (2005). Reinterpreting the development of reading skills. *Reading Research Quarterly, 40*(2), 184–202.

Paulsen, G. (1986). *Hatchet*. MacMillan.

Pearson, P. D., & Gallagher, G. (1983). The gradual release of responsibility model of instruction. *Contemporary Educational Psychology, 8*(3), 112–123.

Perkins, D. N., & Salomon, G. (1992). Transfer of learning. *International encyclopedia of education* (2nd ed.). Pergamon.

Pfost, M., Dörfler, T., & Artelt, C. (2013). Students' extracurricular reading behavior and the development of vocabulary and reading comprehension. *Learning & Individual Differences, 26*, 89–102.

Piaget, J. (1974). *The language and thought of the child*. Meridian.

Portis, A. (2019). *Hey, water!* Neal Porter Books.

Quindlen, A. (2001, September 26). A quilt of a country. *Newsweek*. http://www.newsweek.com/quilt-country-151869

Quirk, M., Schwanenflugel, P. J., & Webb, M. (2009). A short-term longitudinal study of the relationship between motivation to read and reading fluency skill in second grade. *Journal of Literacy Research, 41*(2), 196–227.

RAND Reading Study Group. (2002). *Reading for understanding: Toward an R & D program in reading comprehension* (C. Snow, Chair). Author.

Rapp, D. N., Van den Broek, P., McMaster, K. L., Kendeou, P., & Espin, C. A. (2007). Higher-order comprehension processes in struggling readers: A perspective for research and intervention. *Scientific Studies of Reading, 11*(4), 289–312.

Reynolds, J. (2019). *Look both ways: A tale told in ten blocks*. Simon & Schuster.

Rinehart, S. D., Stahl, S. A., & Erickson, L. G. (1986). Some effects of summarization training on reading and studying. *Reading Research Quarterly, 21*(4), 422–438.

Rosenshine, B., & Meister, C. (1994), Reciprocal teaching: A review of the research. *Review of Educational Research, 64*(4), 479–530.

Ryan, P. M. (1999). *Riding freedom*. Scholastic.

Scarborough, H. S. (2002). Connecting early language and literacy to later reading (dis)abilities: Evidence, theory, and practice. In S. B. Newman & D. K. Dickinson (Eds.), *Handbook of early literacy research* (pp. 97–110). Guilford Press.

Schwartz, A. E., Horn, K. M., Ellen, I. G., & Cordes, S. A. (2020). Do housing vouchers improve academic performance? Evidence from New York City. *Journal of Policy Analysis and Management, 39*(1), 131–158.

Scieszka, J. (1989). *The true story of the three little pigs*. Viking.

Sciurba, K. (2017). Journeys toward textual relevance: Male readers of color and the significance of Malcolm X and Harry Potter. *Journal of Literacy Research, 49*(3), 371–392.

Sendak, M. (1988). *Where the wild things are*. HarperCollins.

Shanahan, T. (2019, September 14). *Why not teach reading comprehension for a change?* Shanahan on Literacy. https://shanahanonliteracy.com/blog/why-not-teach-reading-comprehension-for-a-change

Sharma, S. A., & Christ, T. (2017). (2017). Five steps toward successful culturally relevant text selection and integration. *Reading Teacher, 71*(3), 295–307.

Shreeve, J. (1995, January). What happened to Phineas? *Discover*, pp. 78–79.

Singer, L. M., & Alexander, P. A. (2017). Reading on paper and digitally: What the past decades of empirical research reveal. *Journal of Educational Research, 87*(6), 1007–1041.

Snow, C. E. (2002). *Reading for understanding: Toward a research and development program in reading comprehension*. RAND.

Sparapani, N., Connor, C. M., McLean, L., Wood, T., Toste, J., & Day, S. (2018). Direct and reciprocal effects among social skills, vocabulary, and reading comprehension in first grade. *Contemporary Educational Psychology, 53*, 159–167.

Tarchi, C. (2015). Fostering reading comprehension of expository texts through the activation of readers' prior knowledge and inference-making skills. *International Journal of Educational Research, 72*, 80–88.

Tennyson, R. D., & Cocchiarella, M. J. (1986). An empirically based instructional design theory for teaching concepts. *Review of Educational Research, 56*(1), 40–71.

Thorndike, E. L. (1917). Reading as reasoning: A study of mistakes in paragraph reading. *Journal of Educational Psychology, 8*(6), 323–332.

Tighe, E., & Schatschneider, C. (2014). A dominance analysis approach to determining predictor importance in third, seventh, and tenth grade reading comprehension skills. *Reading & Writing, 27*(1), 101–127.

Torppa, M., Niemi, P., Vasalampi, K., Lerkkanen, M-K., Tolvanen, A., & Poikkeus, A-M. (2019). Leisure reading (but not any kind) and reading comprehension support each other: A longitudinal study across grades 1 and 9. *Child Development, 91*(3), 876–900. https://doi.org/10.1111/cdev.13241

Trzesniewski, K. H., Moffitt, T. E., Caspi, A., Taylor, A., & Maughan, B. (2006). Revisiting the association between reading achievement and antisocial behavior: New evidence of an environmental explanation from a twin study. *Child Development, 77*(1), 72–88.

Vacca, R. T., Vacca, J. L., & Mraz, M. E. (2017). *Content area reading: Literacy and learning across the curriculum* (12th ed.). Pearson.

Valencia, S. W., Wixson, K. K., & Pearson, P. D. (2014). Putting text complexity in context. *Elementary School Journal, 115*(2), 270–289.

Van den Broek, P., Fletcher, C. R., & Risden, K. (1993). Investigations of inferential processes in reading: A theoretical and methodological integration. *Discourse Processes, 16*(1–2), 169–180.

Vygotsky, L. S. (1978). *Mind and society: The development of higher psychological processes.* Harvard University Press.

White, E. B. (1952). *Charlotte's web.* Harper.

Wilkinson, I. A. G., & Nelson, K. (2013). Role of discussion in reading comprehension. In J. Hattie & E. Anderman (Eds.), *International guide to student achievement* (pp. 299–302). Routledge.

Wineburg, S. S. (1991). On the reading of historical texts: Notes on the breach between school and academy. *American Education Research Journal, 28*(3), 495–519.

Wolfe, M. (2001). *Proust and the squid: The story and science of the reading brain.* Harper Perennial.

Wolfe, P. (2001). *Brain matters: Translating research into classroom practice.* ASCD.

Wood, A. (1984). *The napping House.* HMH Books for Young Children.

Woodson, J. (2019). *Red at the bone: A novel.* Riverhead.

Worthy, J., Patterson, E., & Salas, R. (2002). "More than just reading": The human factor in reaching resistant readers. *Reading Research & Instruction, 41*(2), 177–201.

Yang, Y. (2006). Reading strategies or comprehension monitoring strategies? *Reading Psychology, 27*(4), 313–343.

Zusak, M. (2005). *The book thief.* Alfred A. Knopf.

Index

A SAGE Publishing Company

Helping educators make the greatest impact

CORWIN HAS ONE MISSION: to enhance education through intentional professional learning.

We build long-term relationships with our authors, educators, clients, and associations who partner with us to develop and continuously improve the best evidence-based practices that establish and support lifelong learning.

CORWIN Fisher & Frey

> ❝ Every student deserves a great
> teacher—not by chance, but by design. ❞

Read more from Fisher & Frey

DOUGLAS FISHER, NANCY FREY, NANCY AKHAVAN

Tap your intuition, collaborate with your peers, and put the research-based strategies embedded in this roadmap to work in your classroom to implement or deepen a strong, successful balanced literacy program.

DOUGLAS FISHER, NANCY FREY, OLIVIA AMADOR, JOSEPH ASSOF

With cross-curricular examples, planning templates, professional learning questions, and a PLC guide, this is the most practical planner for designing and delivering highly effective instruction.

DOUGLAS FISHER, NANCY FREY, RUSSELL J. QUAGLIA, DOMINIQUE SMITH, LISA L. LANDE

Engagement by Design puts you in control of managing your classroom's success and increasing student learning, one motivated student at a time.

DOUGLAS FISHER, NANCY FREY, DIANE LAPP

In this edition of the best-selling *Text Complexity*, the renowned author team lays open the instructional routines that take students to new places as readers.

DOUGLAS FISHER, NANCY FREY

Nancy Frey and Douglas Fisher articulate an instructional plan for close reading so clearly and so squarely built on research that it's the only resource a teacher will need.

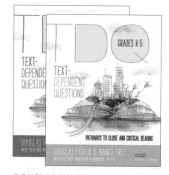

DOUGLAS FISHER, NANCY FREY, HEATHER ANDERSON, MARISOL THAYRE

The authors break down the process into four cognitive pathways that help teachers "organize the journey through a text" and frame an extended discussion around it.

To order your copies, visit corwin.com/FisherandFrey